Great Meals in Minutes

Italian Menus

Great Meals in Minutes was created by Rebus Inc., and published by Time-Life Books.

This edition published 1994 by Bloomsbury Books, an imprint of The Godfrey Cave Group, 42 Bloomsbury Street, London, WC1B 3QJ.

© 1994 Time-Life Books BV.

ISBN 1 85471 571 2

Printed and bound in Great Britain.

Great Meals in Minutes

Italian Menus

Silvana La Rocca

Menu 1
Stuffed Porcini Mushrooms   8
Chicken with Peppers
Radicchio and Mozzarella Salad

Menu 2
Fillets of Sole Signora Concetta   10
Baked Onions
Fresh Tomato Salad

Menu 3
Spicy Lamb Chops   12
Hunter-style Potatoes
Green Beans with Mint

Felice and Lidia Bastianich

Menu 1
Scampi with Quick Risotto   16
Asparagus Gratinati

Menu 2
Quail with Polenta   18
Green Bean, Red Onion, and Bacon Salad

Menu 3
Chicken Felice   21
Swiss Chard and Potatoes

Lynne Kasper

Menu 1
Escarole, Onion, and Coppa Salad   24
Peasant-style Risotto

Menu 2
Renaissance Almond Broth   26
Sweet and Savoury Grilled Lamb
Herb-Roasted Potatoes

Menu 3
Prosciutto and Mostarda di Cremona   29
Minestrone with Chickpeas

Susan DeRege

Menu 1
Piedmontese Pork Medallions   34
Straw and Hay Pasta with Butter Sauce
Carrots with Kirsch

Menu 2
Chicken Breasts Milanese   36
Risotto with Porcini Mushrooms
Endive salad with Green Herb Sauce

Menu 3
Cream of Artichoke Soup   39
Veal Scallopini Cavour
Peperonata

Nancy Verde Barr

Menu 1
Braised Duck with Black Olives   44
Penne with Mushroom Sauce

Menu 2
Piquant Chicken   46
Baked Stuffed Tomatoes

Menu 3
Courgette Soup   49
Lamb Catanzaro-style
Broccoli Rabe

Robert Pucci

Menu 1
Braised Beef Tenderloin in Wine Sauce   54
Potatoes Parmigiana
Sautéed Vegetables

Menu 2
Linguine with Clam Sauce   56
Fillets of Flounder Sorrento
Sautéed Spinach with Pine Nuts and Raisins

Menu 3
Angel Hair Pasta with Onions and Pepper Strips   58
Veal Scallopini Marsala
Warm Vegetable Salad

Bloomsbury Books
London

Silvana La Rocca

Menu 1
(right)
Stuffed Porcini Mushrooms
Chicken with Peppers
Radicchio and Mozzarella Salad

Born into an Italian family that subscribes to the ancient saying *la civiltà sta nel piatto* (civilization can be found on a plate), Silvana La Rocca was exposed to good cooking and fine dining at an early age. Her maternal grandmother taught her how to make fresh pasta; her mother introduced her to the vast diversity of Italian cooking; and her father taught her how to select the freshest ingredients at the market and to prepare them simply in the Abruzzo style.

Still a adherent of Abruzzese cooking, Silvana La Rocca offers three meals featuring dishes and ingredients popular in that region. In Menus 1 and 2 she flavours the entrées, chicken and sole, respectively, with olive oil, garlic, and black pepper – all typical Abruzzese seasonings. She adds white wine and rosemary to the chicken and heightens the flavour of the tomato sauce for the sole with capers. The fish recipe is named for her grandmother.

In Menu 3 she features lamb chops that in Italy are called *agnello brucialingua*, or 'lamb that burns the tongue,' because they are fried with hot chili peppers. According to the cook, the accompanying potatoes (potato wedges baked in their skins with onions and carrots) are often prepared by Abruzzese hunters on trips to the mountains. The green bean and mint salad is a refreshing counterpoint to the spicy lamb.

Note: In all these recipes, tablespoon measurements are level tablespoons unless otherwise stated.

Fresh flowers and a richly patterned cloth set a festive tone for this colourful dinner. Golden-brown chicken pieces tossed with strips of red pepper are the appetizing entrée. Serve the cheese-and-herb-filled porcini mushroom caps and the radicchio and mozzarella salad in separate pottery dishes.

Stuffed Porcini Mushrooms
Chicken with Peppers
Radicchio and Mozzarella Salad

Large-capped meaty *funghi porcini*, called pigs' mushrooms because pigs love their flavour, are prized in Italy as a delicacy. Because *porcini* have a short growing season and are highly perishable, fresh ones may be difficult to locate at a greengrocer or an Italian market. As a substitute, use very large white cultivated mushrooms. Buy mushrooms that are fresh looking, unblemished, and have tightly fitting caps with no gills showing. Mushrooms will keep briefly in the refrigerator in a bowl covered with a damp towel, but they are best used the same day they are bought. Never wash or soak mushrooms; they absorb water and lose their flavour. Simply wipe them clean with a damp paper towel.

What to drink
Choose a full-bodied, very dry white wine such as an Italian Greco di Tufo or Pinot Bianco, or a California Pinot Blanc, for this northern Italian menu.

Start-to-Finish Steps
1 Squeeze lemon juice for mushrooms and salad recipes. Wash parsley and fresh herbs, if using, dry with paper towels, and set aside. Peel garlic for chicken and mushrooms recipes.
2 Follow salad recipe steps 1 through 3.
3 Follow mushrooms recipe steps 1 through 7.
4 Follow chicken recipe steps 1 through 5.
5 While chicken is browning, follow mushrooms recipe step 8 and salad recipe step 4.
6 Follow chicken recipe steps 6 through 8.
7 While chicken bakes, follow mushrooms recipe step 9 and serve as an appetizer.
8 Follow salad recipe step 5, chicken recipe step 9, and serve.

Stuffed Porcini Mushrooms

4 large fresh porcini mushrooms, or 4 extra-large cultivated mushrooms (about 125 g (4 oz) total weight)
Small bunch fresh parsley
60 g (2 oz) Parmesan cheese, preferably imported
60 g (2 oz) tin flat oil-packed anchovy fillets
1 clove garlic, peeled
4 fresh basil leaves, or 1 tablespoon dried
2 tablespoons lemon juice
1 teaspoon freshly ground black pepper
4 tablespoons olive oil

1 Preheat oven to 190°C (375°F or Mark 5).
2 Wipe mushrooms with damp cloth or paper towel. Carefully remove stems and reserve. Place mushrooms cap-side down in small baking dish; set aside.
3 Remove stems from parsley, and coarsely chop enough sprigs to measure 15 g (1/2 oz). Reserve remaining sprigs for garnish, if desired.
4 Using food processor or grater, grate enough Parmesan to measure 30 g (1 oz).
5 Drain 4 anchovy fillets and set aside; reserve oil and remaining fillets for another use.
6 In food processor or blender, combine mushroom stems, garlic, basil, anchovy fillets, Parmesan, lemon juice, parsley, and black pepper. Process 45 seconds. Scrape down sides of bowl and process another 30 seconds, or until mixture is medium-coarse.
7 Divide filling among mushroom caps, spoon 1 tablespoon olive oil over each mushroom, and set aside.
8 Place mushrooms in oven and bake 12 to 15 minutes, or until filling shrinks away slightly from sides of caps.
9 Transfer mushrooms to serving dish and garnish with parsley, if desired.

Chicken with Peppers

1.25–1.5 Kg (2 1/2–3 lbs) chicken parts
125 g (4 oz) plain flour
Salt
2 sprigs fresh rosemary, or 1 1/2 tablespoons dried
100 ml (3 fl oz) olive oil
2 to 3 cloves garlic, peeled
2 medium-size red bell peppers (about 250 g (8 oz) total weight)
125 ml (4 fl oz) dry white wine or dry vermouth
Freshly ground black pepper

1 Rinse chicken under cold running water and dry thoroughly with paper towels. Place flour in pie pan or plate. Sprinkle chicken with salt and lightly

dredge each piece in flour, coating evenly; shake off excess and set aside. Chop rosemary sprigs and set aside.

2   In large heavy-gauge skillet, heat olive oil over medium-high heat. Add garlic and sauté, stirring occasionally, 2 to 3 minutes, or until golden brown.

3   Remove garlic and discard. Place chicken in skillet in single layer, skin side down, increase heat to high, and sauté until one side is golden brown, 3 to 4 minutes.

4   While chicken is browning, halve, core, and seed bell peppers. Cut into 5 mm (¼ inch) strips and set aside.

5   Turn chicken with tongs and sauté other side until evenly browned, 3 to 4 minutes. Meanwhile, lightly oil roasting pan.

6   Remove skillet from heat and transfer chicken pieces to roasting pan. Pour off fat from skillet, leaving about 2 tablespoons, and return skillet to medium heat. Add wine, increase heat to medium-high, and boil for 1 to 2 minutes, or until liquid is reduced by half.

7   Lower heat to medium, add bell pepper strips and rosemary, and cook, stirring, another 2 minutes.

8   Spoon bell pepper mixture over chicken pieces, sprinkle with freshly ground black pepper to taste, and bake, uncovered, in preheated 190°C (375°F or Mark 5) oven 15 minutes.

9   Transfer chicken and peppers to platter and serve.

Radicchio and Mozzarella Salad

2 to 3 heads radicchio (about 350 g (12 oz) total weight)
250 g (8 oz) fresh mozzarella, or good quality packaged mozzarella
7 fresh mint leaves, or ½ teaspoon dried
2 to 3 tablespoons lemon juice
100 ml (3 fl oz) olive oil
Salt and freshly ground black pepper

1   Wash radicchio and discard any bruised or wilted leaves. Dry with paper towels and place in salad bowl.

2   Cut cheese into thin 3½ cm (1½ inch) long strips and place on top of radicchio.

3   If using fresh mint, tear leaves into small pieces and sprinkle over salad. (If using dried, do not add at this point.) Cover bowl with plastic wrap and refrigerate until ready to serve.

4   In a small bowl, combine lemon juice, olive oil, and dried mint, if using. Add salt and pepper to

taste and, with fork, stir dressing until blended; set aside.

5   Just before serving, stir dressing to recombine, add to salad, and toss gently.

Added touch
For this dessert, select fresh figs that are medium-soft and that exude a drop of liquid from the rounded blossom end.

Fresh Figs in Monks' Robes

8 large fresh figs with smooth skins (about 750 g (1½ lb) total weight)
8 blanched almonds
100 g (3 oz) unsweetened cocoa powder
175 g (6 oz) confectioners' sugar

1   Peel each fig carefully: Holding fig pointed end down, make shallow crosswise incision with paring knife just beneath skin at rounded end. Holding skin firmly against blade with your thumb, run knife under skin while gently pulling downward in the same motion. Repeat until all skin is removed.

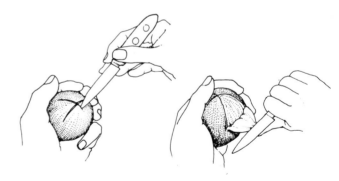

2   Press a whole blanched almond into bottom of each fig until totally enclosed.

3   Sift cocoa and sugar together into shallow dish.

4   Roll each fig in cocoa-sugar mixture until evenly coated.

5   Place figs on small platter, cover, and refrigerate for 15 to 20 minutes before serving.

Fillets of Sole Signora Concetta
Baked Onions
Fresh Tomato Salad

Special brine-cured olives garnish the sole fillets. The cook suggests using either tiny Italian Gaeta olives or Niçoise olives from France, which range in colour from brown to purple to black.

What to drink

The fresh, lively flavours of these dishes suggest a crisp, dry white wine as an accompaniment. A Verdicchio or Pinot Grigio would do very well, as would a California Sauvignon Blanc.

Start-to-Finish Steps

1 Follow onions recipe steps 1 and 2.
2 Follow sole recipe steps 1 and 2.
3 Follow onions recipe step 3.
4 While onion is cooking, follow salad recipe step 1.
5 Follow onions recipe step 4.
6 Follow sole recipe steps 3 and 4.

7 Follow onions recipe steps 5 and 6.
8 While onions bake, follow salad recipe step 2.
9 Follow sole recipe steps 5 through 9.
10 While sauce for sole is being reheated, follow onions recipe step 7 and salad recipe steps 3 and 4.
11 Follow sole recipe step 10, onions recipe step 8, and serve with salad.

Fillets of Sole Signora Concetta

2 cloves garlic, peeled and chopped
Small bunch fresh basil, or 2 teaspoons dried
500 g (1 lb) can plum tomatoes, drained
2 tablespoons capers

Sole fillets are crescents of baked onion look dramatic against solid black plates. The tomato salad adds extra colour.

125 ml (4 fl oz) olive oil
125 ml (4 fl oz) dry white wine or dry vermouth
Salt and freshly ground black pepper
4 medium-size fillets of sole
100 g (3 oz) plain flour
125 g (4 oz) Parmesan cheese
60 g (2 oz) small dark olives, preferably Gaeta or
  Niçoise

1 If using fresh basil, rinse and pat dry. Reserve 5 or
   6 leaves and refrigerate remainder for another use.
2 Coarsely chop enough tomatoes to measure 350 g
   (12 oz) reserving remainder for another use. Drain
   capers.
3 In medium-size non aluminium skillet, heat 4
   tablespoons olive oil over medium-high heat. Add
   garlic and sauté 2 to 3 minutes, or until golden.
4 Add tomatoes, basil, capers, and wine to skillet,
   and stir to combine. Raise heat to high and quickly
   bring sauce to a boil. Remove skillet from heat
   immediately, add salt and pepper to taste, and set
   aside.
5 Rinse fillets under cold water and dry with paper
   towels. Place flour on sheet of waxed paper.
   Sprinkle both sides of fillets with salt and pepper.
   Dredge fillets in flour, making sure each piece is
   well coated; shake off excess.
6 In large heavy-gauge non-aluminium skillet, heat
   remaining olive oil over medium-high heat. When
   oil is hot, add fillets, arranging in single layer, and
   lightly brown on one side, about 4 minutes.
7 Meanwhile, grate enough Parmesan to measure
   60 g (2 oz). Remove pits from olives; set aside.
8 Turn fish and brown another 4 minutes.
9 Return sauce to medium heat and warm 2 to 3
   minutes.
10 Divide fish among dinner plates. Top each fillet
   with hot tomato sauce, sprinkle with freshly grated
   Parmesan, and garnish with black olives.

3 Cut off root end of onion and peel. Plunge onion
   into boiling water and boil 5 minutes.
4 Transfer onion to colander, drain, and set aside to
   cool.
5 Peel and quarter onion; cut quarters into thirds and
   arrange in single layer in baking dish. Sprinkle
   with sugar, fennel seeds, and salt and pepper to
   taste. Drizzle with olive oil and toss onions until
   coated.
6 Bake 30 to 35 minutes, or until onions are light
   golden.
7 Remove from oven and allow to cool 5 to 6
   minutes.
8 Sprinkle onions with vinegar and divide among
   plates.

Fresh Tomato Salad

4 large tomatoes (about 1½ Kg (3 lb) total weight),
  washed
4 scallions, washed, trimmed, and chopped
5 sprigs parsley, washed and chopped
Large lemon, washed
1 teaspoon dried oregano
Salt and freshly ground black pepper
125 ml (4 fl oz) olive oil

1 Cut tomatoes into eighths or narrow wedges and
   place in large bowl. Add scallions and parsley to
   tomatoes.
2 Holding lemon over bowl with tomatoes, remove
   zest, allowing it to fall into bowl.
3 Cut lemon in half and squeeze enough juice to
   measure 3 tablespoons; add to tomatoes.
4 Season tomatoes with oregano and salt and pepper
   to taste, drizzle with olive oil, and toss gently.
   Adjust seasoning, toss again, and divide among
   individual salad plates.

Baked Onions

Extra-large onion (about 750 g (1½ lb))
1 tablespoon sugar
2 teaspoons fennel seeds
Salt and freshly ground white pepper
4 tablespoons olive oil
2 tablespoons white wine vinegar

1 Preheat oven to 200°C (400°F or Mark 6).
2 In large saucepan, bring 2½ ltrs (4 pts) water to a
   boil over high heat.

<table>
<tr><td>

Menu

3
</td><td>

Spicy Lamb Chops
Hunter-style Potatoes
Green Beans with Mint
</td></tr>
</table>

For the lamb recipe, use fresh hot chilies. Take special care when handling chilies; they contain a highly irritating substance that can burn the skin or cause a rash. Wear thin rubber gloves while working with chilies. After removing the gloves, do not touch your face until you have thoroughly washed your hands with soap and warm water.

What to drink

You will need a sturdy red wine to stand up to the lamb. A Chianti Classico Riserva would be ideal, or try an Italian Taurasi or a California Cabernet Sauvignon.

Start-to-Finish Steps

1 Prepare fresh herbs, if using.
2 Follow potatoes recipe steps 1 and 2.
3 Follow green beans recipe steps 1 through 3.
4 Follow potatoes recipe steps 3 and 4.
5 Follow green beans recipe step 4 and lamb recipe steps 1 through 5.
6 Follow potatoes recipe step 5 and green beans recipe steps 5 and 6.
7 Follow lamb recipe step 6.
8 Follow potatoes recipe step 6, lamb recipe step 7, and serve with green beans.

Serve each of your guests a lamb chop garnished with a chili pepper and sage, some roasted vegetables, and a bean salad.

12

Spicy Lamb Chops

4 fresh hot chili peppers, or 1½ to 3 tablespoons red pepper flakes
2 to 4 cloves garlic, peeled
125 ml (4 fl oz) olive oil
Four 3 cm (1¼ inch) thick loin lamb chops (about 750 g (1½ lb) total weight)
6 to 8 fresh sage leaves, chopped, or ½ teaspoon dried
2 tablespoons white wine vinegar
Salt and freshly ground black pepper
125 ml (4 fl oz) dry white wine or dry vermouth

1   If using fresh chili peppers, rinse under cold running water and dry with paper towels. Wearing rubber gloves, halve peppers lengthwise, remove seeds, and discard.
2   In large heavy-gauge skillet, heat olive oil over medium-high heat. Add chili peppers and garlic, and sauté 2 to 3 minutes, or until garlic is golden. Discard garlic.
3   Add lamb chops to skillet with chili peppers and brown over medium-high heat 3 to 4 minutes on one side.
4   Turn chops and brown another 3 to 4 minutes.
5   Add sage, vinegar, and salt and pepper to taste. Lower heat to medium, turn chops, and cook, uncovered, 8 minutes for rare, 10 for medium, or 12 for well done.
6   Add wine, raise heat to high, and cook chops another 3 to 5 minutes, or until most of wine has evaporated.
7   Divide chops among dinner plates, top each with a spoonful of pan juice, and serve.

Hunter-style Potatoes

4 medium-size boiling potatoes (about 750 g (1½ lb) total weight)
4 medium-size carrots (about 500 g (1 lb) total weight)
2 medium-size yellow onions (about 500 g (1 lb) total weight)
8 cloves garlic
1 tablespoon dried rosemary
Salt and freshly ground black pepper
4 tablespoons olive oil

1   Preheat oven to 200°C (400°F or Mark 6).
2   Wash and dry potatoes; cut into 2½ cm (1 inch) thick wedges. Trim and peel carrots. Halve carrots lengthwise, then cut into 2½ cm (1 inch) long strips. Peel and quarter onions.
3   Combine vegetables in baking dish. Add whole, unpeeled garlic cloves, rosemary, and salt and pepper to taste. Drizzle vegetables with olive oil and toss until well coated.
4   Roast potatoes in upper third of oven 15 minutes.
5   Remove dish from oven, turn vegetables, and return dish to oven. Roast another 15 minutes, or until potatoes are tender when pricked with a sharp knife.
6   Divide vegetables among dinner plates.

Green Beans with Mint

Salt
500 g (1 lb) green beans
1 lemon
10 to 12 fresh mint leaves, shredded, or 1 teaspoon dried
Freshly ground white pepper
100 ml (3 fl oz) olive oil

1   In stockpot or large kettle, bring 4½ ltrs (8 pts) of water and 1 tablespoon salt to a boil over high heat.
2   Meanwhile, snap off ends of beans and discard. Wash beans in cold running water and set aside. Squeeze enough lemon to measure about 3 tablespoons juice.
3   Add beans all at once to boiling water. When water returns to a boil, lower heat to medium-high and cook, uncovered, 7 minutes, or until beans are crisp-tender.
4   Turn beans into colander and refresh under cold running water. Drain and set aside until cool.
5   Dry beans thoroughly with paper towels and transfer to serving bowl. Add dried mint, if using, and white pepper to taste. Toss beans with olive oil until thoroughly coated. Add lemon juice, adjust seasoning, and toss again.
6   Add fresh mint, if using, and divide beans among individual salad plates.

Felice and Lidia Bastianich

Menu 1
(*left*)
Scampi with Quick Risotto
Asparagus Gratinati

Cooking comes naturally to Felice and Lidia Bastianich. As a youth he worked at his father's small northern Italian inn, and from the age of 14, she cooked for her entire family. Advocates of using only top-quality ingredients, the Bastianiches plan meals – both at home and in their restaurant – around what is best in the marketplace, then fill in with their own homemade prosciutto and pasta. By adhering to the unpretentious cooking traditions of their native Istria, the Bastianiches serve meals that are simple and nourishing. As Lidia Bastianich says, 'We want our customers and guests to be able to duplicate our recipes, so we stick to uncomplicated foods and methods.'

Istrian simplicity underlies each of the menus they present here. The sautéed shrimp of Menu 1 are lightly seasoned with garlic, lemon juice, and white wine, and are served on a bed of risotto. The asparagus spears are broiled with a light coating of melted butter and grated Parmesan.

In Istria, where game is abundant, cooks often serve polenta with wild fowl. Menu 2 offers quail in a tomato sauce flavoured with bay leaves, rosemary, and cloves, presented on a platter with polenta. A green bean and bacon salad adds colour and texture to this cold-weather meal.

Chicken is the entrée for Menu 3. The breasts are dredged with flour, dipped in parsley and grated Parmesan, and then sautéed in stock with wine and lemon juice. A substantial dish of Swiss chard and potatoes complements the fowl.

A heaping platter of risotto topped with whole shrimp in a garlic and parsley sauce is a delightful entrée for an informal spring dinner. The crisp-tender asparagus spears should be served on a warmed platter.

Scampi with Quick Risotto
Asparagus Gratinati

When buying raw shrimp, select those that are plump and odour-free; avoid any with meat that has shrunk away from the shell, which indicates that the shrimp have been frozen and thawed. If the shrimp do not have the shells and veins removed, follow step 1 of the recipe. Because they are highly perishable, shrimp should be purchased at the last minute. If you must store them, do so in a covered container in the coldest part of the refrigerator. After cooking, the shrimp should be firm and crisp.

What to drink
A well-chilled fruity white wine such as an Italian Chardonnay or Vernaccia, or a California Sauvignon Blanc or Riesling, goes well with the scampi.

Start-to-Finish Steps
1 Grate enough Parmesan to measure 1 cup for risotto recipe and ¹/₂ cup for asparagus recipe.
2 Follow scampi recipe steps 1 and 2.
3 Follow asparagus recipe steps 1 through 3 and scampi recipe step 3.
4 Follow asparagus recipe step 4 and risotto recipe steps 1 through 3.
5 Follow asparagus recipe steps 5 through 7.
6 Follow risotto recipe steps 4 and 5, and scampi recipe steps 4 through 6.
7 Follow asparagus recipe step 8 and scampi recipe step 7.
8 Follow risotto recipe step 6, scampi recipe step 8, and serve with asparagus.

1 Pinch off legs of shrimp, several at a time, then bend back and snap off sharp, beak-like pieces of shell just above tail. Remove shell and discard. Using sharp paring knife, make shallow incision along back of each shrimp, exposing digestive vein. Extract vein and discard (see illustration).
2 Place shrimp in colander, rinse under cold running water, drain, and dry with paper towels. Set aside.
3 Peel and finely chop garlic. Rinse parsley, dry, and chop enough to measure 3 tablespoons. Squeeze enough lemon juice to measure 2 tablespoons; set aside.
4 In large heavy-gauge skillet, heat olive oil over medium-high heat. Add shrimp and sauté, stirring, about 2 minutes, or until slightly golden.
5 Stir in garlic and sauté 3 minutes, or until golden.
6 Add butter, lemon juice, white wine, and salt and pepper to taste, and cook about 5 minutes, or until shrimp begin to curl and turn opaque.
7 Sprinkle shrimp with parsley and bread crumbs, and cook another minute.
8 Turn shrimp and sauce onto platter with risotto.

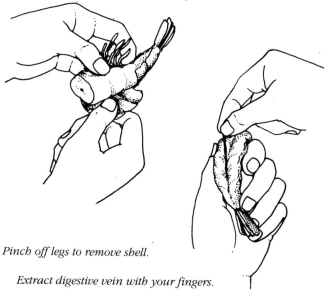

Pinch off legs to remove shell.

Extract digestive vein with your fingers.

Scampi with Quick Risotto

24 large shrimp (about 625 g (1¹/₄ lb) total weight)
4 cloves garlic
Small bunch parsley
1 lemon
3 tablespoons olive oil
4 tablespoons unsalted butter
125 ml (4 fl oz) dry white wine
Salt and freshly ground black pepper
3 tablespoons dry bread crumbs
Quick Risotto (see following recipe)

Quick Risotto

Medium-size yellow onion
2 tablespoons olive oil
350 g (12 oz) long-grain rice

16

4 tablespoons unsalted butter
750 ml–1¼ ltrs (1½–2 pts) chicken stock
Salt and freshly ground black pepper
125 g (4 oz) freshly grated Parmesan cheese

1 Peel and chop onion.
2 In large heavy-gauge saucepan, heat oil over medium-high heat. Add onion and sauté 5 minutes, or until golden.
3 Stir in rice, butter, 750 ml (1½ pts) chicken stock, and salt and pepper to taste. Reduce heat to low, cover, and cook, stirring occasionally, 10 minutes. If rice sticks to pan, add small amounts of stock, stirring after each addition until incorporated.
4 After 10 minutes, remove cover and allow excess stock to boil off; or, if rice seems too dry, add small amounts of stock, cover, and continue simmering another 5 to 10 minutes, or until rice is tender and all liquid is absorbed. Keep pan covered until ready to serve.
5 Meanwhile, place serving platter under hot running water to warm.
6 When ready to serve, dry platter. Add Parmesan to rice and stir until combined. Turn out onto warm platter.

Asparagus Gratinati

16 medium-size asparagus spears (about 500 g (1 lb) total weight)
2 tablespoons unsalted butter
60 g (2 oz) freshly grated Parmesan cheese

1 In stockpot or large saucepan, bring 1¼ ltrs (2 pts) of water to a boil over high heat.
2 Meanwhile, rinse asparagus under cold running water and drain. Trim off woody stems and, if desired, peel.
3 Using kitchen string, tie asparagus into 2 bundles. Stand upright in pot, cover, and cook over high heat 6 minutes, or until crisp-tender.
4 With tongs, transfer bundles to colander, untie, and let cool.
5 In small heavy-gauge saucepan or butter warmer, melt butter over low heat.
6 In flameproof baking dish, arrange asparagus spears side by side in single layer and drizzle with melted butter. Sprinkle with Parmesan and set aside.
7 Preheat broiler.
8 Before serving, broil asparagus about 4 inches from heating element 3 to 5 minutes, or just until cheese turns light golden.

Added touch
When you ignite the warmed brandy Grand Marnier to flambé the strawberries, the flames may be high at first but should die down quickly. If they do not subside, simply put a cover on the skillet.

Flamed Strawberries

500 g (1 lb) fresh strawberries
Large orange
250 ml (8 fl oz) heavy cream
60 g (2 oz) sugar
2 tablespoons Grand Marnier or other orange liqueur
2 tablespoons brandy
500 ml (1 pt) vanilla ice cream

1 Place medium-size bowl and beaters in freezer to chill.
2 Rinse strawberries and pat dry with paper towels. With sharp paring knife, hull berries and set aside.
3 Rinse orange and dry. Grate enough rind to measure about 3 tablespoons. Cut orange in half. Squeeze juice from one half, reserving remaining half for another use.
4 Pour heavy cream into chilled bowl and whip with electric mixer at high speed until stiff. Cover and refrigerate.
5 In small heavy-gauge skillet, heat sugar over medium heat, stirring, until melted and golden, about 5 minutes.
6 Stir orange rind into sugar and cook about 2 minutes, or until sugar is light brown and syrupy.
7 Add strawberries, orange juice, Grand Marnier, and brandy, and stir to combine. Simmer gently, turning berries to coat with syrup, another 3 minutes.
8 Remove skillet from heat and, averting your face, ignite syrup. When flames have subsided, set skillet aside.
9 Place a generous spoonful of whipped cream in centre of each of 4 dessert plates. Top each with a scoop of ice cream and surround 'islands' with strawberries. Spoon remaining syrup over ice cream and serve.

Quail with Polenta
Green Bean, Red Onion, and Bacon Salad

A popular game bird considered a delicacy throughout the world, quail has pale-coloured flesh that tastes like a gamey version of dark-meat chicken. Fresh quail are now available year-round at many butchers. When buying quail, select those that are plump and silky-skinned with no discolouration.

What to drink
For this cold-weather meal, the cooks suggest a full-bodied red Barolo or Barbaresco from the Italian Piedmont or a Merlot from Friuli. California Merlot is a good domestic alternative.

Start-to-Finish Steps
1 Coarsely chop bacon for quail and salad recipes.
2 Follow salad recipe steps 1 through 3.
3 Follow quail recipe steps 1 and 2.
4 Follow salad recipe step 4 and polenta recipe steps 1 and 2.
5 Follow quail recipe steps 3 through 5.
6 While quail browns, follow salad recipe steps 5 through 8.
7 Follow quail recipe steps 6 and 7.
8 Follow polenta recipe steps 3 through 5.
9 Follow quail recipe step 8 and serve with polenta and salad.

Arrange the sautéed quail attractively around the polenta and garnish with a sprig of parsley, if desired; extra sauce may be served on the side. Bacon and red onion rings add colour to the green beans.

Quail with Polenta

2 medium-size yellow onions (about 500 g (1 lb) total weight)
Small bunch fresh rosemary, or ¹/₂ teaspoon dried
125 ml (4 fl oz) olive or vegetable oil
2 slices bacon, coarsely chopped
4 cloves
3 bay leaves
Salt
Freshly ground black pepper
8 quail (about 1.75 Kg (3¹/₂ lb) total weight)
60 g (2 oz) Parmesan cheese (optional)
2 teaspoons tomato paste
250 ml (8 fl oz) dry white wine
500 ml (1 pt) chicken stock
Polenta (see following recipe)

1 Peel and dice onions. Rinse fresh rosemary and pat dry with paper towels. Chop enough to measure 1 teaspoon.

2 In large heavy-gauge skillet, heat oil over medium heat. Add onions, rosemary, bacon, cloves, bay leaves, and salt and pepper to taste, and sauté, stirring occasionally, 5 to 10 minutes, or until onions are nicely browned.

3 Add quail and brown 8 to 10 minutes on one side.

4 If using Parmesan, grate enough in food processor or with grater to measure 30 g (1 oz); set aside.

5 Turn birds and cook another 8 to 10 minutes on other side, or until evenly browned.

6 In small bowl, blend tomato paste and wine. Add mixture to skillet and stir into pan juices until blended, basting birds as you stir. Raise heat to medium-high and simmer until liquid has almost evaporated, about 12 minutes.

7 Add stock and simmer another 15 minutes, or until tip of knife easily penetrates breast and juices run clear.

8 Transfer birds to platter with polenta. Pour sauce through strainer set over sauceboat or small bowl, extruding as much liquid as possible with back of spoon. Spoon sauce over each bird and around polenta. Sprinkle birds with cheese, if using, and serve with remaining sauce.

Polenta

125 g (4 oz) coarsely ground cornmeal
1/2 teaspoon salt
3 tablespoons unsalted butter
4 or 5 bay leaves

1 Preheat oven to 100°C (200°F or SLOW).

2 In large heavy-gauge saucepan, bring 1 ltr (1³/₄ pts) water to a boil over high heat.

3 Place serving platter in oven to warm.

4 Reduce heat under saucepan to medium and add cornmeal in a very slow, steady stream, stirring constantly with wooden spoon. Add salt, butter, and bay leaves, and continue stirring until polenta thickens and pulls away from sides of pan, about 15 minutes.

5 Remove bay leaves and discard. With rubber spatula, turn out polenta into middle of warm platter.

Green Bean, Red Onion, and Bacon Salad

500 g (1 lb) green beans
Small red onion
4 slices bacon, coarsely chopped
3 tablespoons white or red wine vinegar
3 tablespoons olive or vegetable oil, approximately
Salt and freshly ground black pepper

1 In medium-size saucepan, bring 2¹/₂ ltrs (4 pts) of water to a boil over high heat.

2 Meanwhile, trim beans. Peel red onion and cut into thin slices. Separate into rings and set aside.

3 Add beans to boiling water, lower heat to medium, cover, and cook 5 minutes, or just until crisp-tender.

4 Turn beans into colander and refresh under cold running water. Drain and set aside to cool.

5 In small skillet, cook bacon over medium heat, stirring occasionally, 5 minutes, or until crisp.

6 Meanwhile, transfer beans to large bowl.

7 Remove skillet from heat and pour off bacon fat. Add vinegar, stir, and return to heat for 1 minute.

8 Pour bacon and vinegar mixture over beans, add oil and salt and pepper to taste, and toss until combined. Adjust seasoning, toss again, and arrange on serving platter. Top with onion rings and set aside until ready to serve.

<table>
<tr><td>

Menu
3

</td><td>

Chicken Felice
Swiss Chard and Potatoes

</td></tr>
</table>

The lemony, cheese-encrusted boneless chicken breasts are simple to prepare and are an impressive dinner for company. The vegetable dish of Swiss chard and coarsely mashed potatoes can be varied if you wish: Substitute spinach or savoy cabbage for the chard.

For the best flavour, you should always buy Parmesan cheese by the chunk and grate it at home as needed. Slice off the rind before grating. If you are using a food processor to grate the cheese, cut the cheese into 1 cm ($^1/_2$ inch) cubes before grating with the steel blade.

What to drink

A dry, lightly acidic white Pinot Grigio, Gavi, or Verdicchio would be good here, or choose a domestic Sauvignon Blanc or fully dry Chenin Blanc.

Start-to-Finish Steps

1 Follow Swiss chard recipe steps 1 through 4.
2 Follow chicken recipe steps 1 through 3.
3 Follow Swiss chard recipe step 5.
4 Follow chicken recipe steps 4 through 6.
5 Follow Swiss chard recipe step 6.
6 Follow chicken recipe steps 7 through 10.
7 Follow Swiss chard recipe steps 7 through 10.
8 Follow chicken recipe steps 11 and 12 and Swiss chard recipe step 11.
9 Follow chicken recipe steps 13 and 14, and serve with Swiss chard and potatoes.

Chicken Felice

4 tablespoons unsalted butter
Small bunch parsley
60 g (2 oz) Parmesan cheese
4 skinless, boneless chicken breasts (about 750 g
    (1$^1/_2$ lb) total weight), halved and pounded 5 mm
    ($^1/_4$ inch) thick
4 eggs

Crisp golden chicken breasts topped with a lemon and wine sauce are accompanied by Swiss chard mashed with potatoes.

4 tablespoons milk
Salt and freshly ground black pepper
125 ml (4 fl oz) vegetable oil
125 g (4 oz) plain flour
3 lemons
250 ml (8 fl oz) dry white wine
750 ml (1½ pts) chicken stock

1   Preheat oven to 100°C (200°F or SLOW). Set out butter to reach room temperature.
2   Wash and dry parsley; chop enough to measure 2 tablespoons and refrigerate remainder for another use. In food processor fitted with steel blade, or with grater, grate enough cheese to measure 60 g (2 oz); set aside.
3   Rinse chicken and dry with paper towels.
4   Beat eggs in medium-size bowl. Add milk, grated cheese, chopped parsley, and salt and pepper to taste, and stir to combine.
5   In large heavy-gauge skillet, heat vegetable oil over medium-high heat until hot but not smoking.
6   Place flour in pie pan. One by one, dredge each breast lightly with flour, shake off excess, and dip in egg and cheese mixture, letting excess mixture drip off into bowl. Place coated breasts in skillet and fry 5 minutes on one side, or until golden.
7   Meanwhile, line heatproof platter with double thickness of paper towels. Rinse 2 lemons and dry. Cut each lemon into rounds, then halve, and set aside. Squeeze enough juice from remaining lemon to measure 2 tablespoons.
8   With tongs, turn breasts and fry another 5 minutes on other side, or until golden.
9   Transfer chicken to paper-towel-lined platter, loosely cover with foil, and keep warm in oven.
10 Pour off oil from skillet. Add wine, lemon juice, stock, and salt and pepper to taste to skillet and bring to a boil over medium-high heat. Continue boiling until sauce is reduced to about 250 ml (8 fl oz), about 10 to 15 minutes.
11 Place 4 dinner plates in oven to warm.
12 Reduce heat under skillet to medium. Return chicken to skillet and simmer 15 minutes.
13 Transfer chicken to warm plates. Add butter, 1 tablespoon at a time, to liquid in pan, swirling after each addition until butter is incorporated.
14 Remove pan from heat. Top each breast with a generous spoonful of sauce and garnish with lemon slices.

Swiss Chard and Potatoes

2 bunches Swiss chard (about 2 Kg (4 lb) total weight)
3 medium-size potatoes (about 625 g (1¼ lb) total weight)
4 cloves garlic
4 tablespoons olive oil
3 tablespoons unsalted butter
Salt and freshly ground black pepper

1   In stockpot or large kettle, bring 7 ltrs (12 pts) of water to a boil over high heat.
2   Meanwhile, trim off lower (stem) half of Swiss chard. Cut leaf tops into 2½ cm (1 inch) pieces and wash thoroughly in several changes of cold water to remove all traces of grit.
3   Peel and quarter potatoes.
4   Add potatoes to boiling water and cook 5 minutes.
5   Add Swiss chard to potatoes and cook another 10 minutes.
6   Transfer vegetables to colander and drain.
7   Bruise garlic cloves with flat side of knife blade and peel.
8   In large heavy-gauge saucepan, heat oil over medium heat. Add garlic and sauté, stirring occasionally, until browned, 2 to 3 minutes.
9   Add Swiss chard, potatoes, butter, and salt and pepper to taste, and mash coarsely.
10 Cook mixture, stirring constantly with wooden spoon, 5 minutes.
11 Remove garlic cloves and discard. Turn vegetables into large heatproof bowl and keep warm in SLOW oven until ready to serve.

Lynne Kasper

Menu 1
(*right*)
Escarole, Onion, and Coppa Salad
Peasant-style Risotto

Lynne Kasper began her food career studying classic French theory and technique. but has amplified her food knowledge by researching Italian cuisine and history in Europe. Well versed in Italian cooking methods, she nonetheless describes herself as an interpretive cook who likes to vary traditional recipes but still preserve the essence of the originals.

For the risotto of Menu 1, a mainstay of the northern Piedmontese winter diet, she short-cuts the standard lengthy cooking process by covering the risotto while it cooks and stirring it only to prevent sticking. The result is still delicious and creamy.

Menu 2 is in the Renaissance style: The almond broth and broiled leg of lamb both incorporate the sweet, spicy, and savoury flavours loved by sixteenth-century cooks. However, Lynne Kasper serves the lamb rare to medium-rare rather than in the traditionally favoured well-done style. Roasted potatoes go well with the lamb.

Menu 3, a country-style meal that is good on a chilly autumn or winter day, features a first course of prosciutto with *mostarda di Cremona*, a spicy fruit relish imported from Cremona in Lombardy. The main course is a rich minestrone from the Marches region, served with crusty Italian bread.

Serve your guests the refreshing escarole, red onion, and coppa salad as a first course, and while they are enjoying it, finish preparing the peasant-style risotto.

Escarole, Onion, and Coppa Salad
Peasant-style Risotto

The light prelude to this substantial meal is a simple salad of escarole, onion, and *coppa*. A member of the endive family, escarole has a bushy head with broad, slightly curled, dark green leaves. If you plan to store the escarole for several days before using it, leave the head intact, place it in a plastic bag, and store in the refrigerator; wash just before using. You may wish to vary this salad by adding chopped bell peppers, marinated mushrooms, and quartered artichoke hearts. To dress the salad, the cook suggests a flavourful extra-virgin olive oil, particularly one from Tuscany or Liguria.

What to drink
The hearty main dish needs a medium-bodied red wine with a good flavour. The cook likes Barbera d'Alba, but a Barbera d'Asti, a Dolcetto, or a California Zinfandel is also fine.

Start-to-Finish Steps
1   Rinse fresh herbs, if using, and pat dry with paper towels. Chop basil for salad recipe; chop enough marjoram to measure 2 teaspoons for risotto recipe.
2   Follow risotto recipe steps 1 through 9.
3   While rice is cooking, follow salad recipe steps 1 through 3.
4   Follow risotto recipe steps 10 through 12.
5   While risotto is resting, follow salad recipe steps 4 and 5 and serve.
6   Follow risotto recipe steps 13 and 14, and serve.

Escarole, Onion, and Coppa Salad

Medium-size head escarole
Medium-size red onion
60 g (2 oz) sliced sweet coppa or capocollo
30 g (1 oz) sliced hot coppa or capocollo
6 tablespoons extra-virgin olive oil, approximately
2 tablespoons good-quality red or white wine vinegar, approximately
8 fresh basil leaves, chopped, or 1/2 teaspoon dried, approximately
Salt
Freshly ground black pepper

1   Remove any tough or bruised outer leaves from escarole. Wash escarole and dry in salad spinner or with paper towels. Tear into bite-sized pieces and place in large salad bowl.
2   Peel and thinly slice onion. Add to escarole, cover bowl with plastic wrap, and refrigerate until ready to serve.
3   Coarsely chop coppa or capocollo; set aside.
4   Just before serving, add olive oil, vinegar, basil, and salt and pepper to taste. Toss salad to combine, taste, and adjust seasoning, adding more oil or vinegar, if desired.
5   Add coppa or capocollo to salad and toss to combine.

Peasant-style Risotto

2 medium-size carrots (about 350 g (12 oz) total weight)
2 medium-size yellow onions (about 500 g (1 lb) total weight)
Small head cabbage (about 500 g (1 lb))
625 g (1 1/4 lb) mild home-style Italian sausage
2 tablespoons vegetable oil
250 g (8 oz) canned Italian plum tomatoes
Large clove garlic
2 bay leaves
1 sprig fresh rosemary, or 1/2 teaspoon dried
2 teaspoons fresh marjoram, chopped, or 1/2 teaspoon dried
1 1/4 ltr (2 pts) chicken or beef stock, approximately
500 g (1 lb) canned pinto beans
175 ml (6 fl oz) dry red wine
250 g (8 oz) Italian Arborio rice
Salt and freshly ground black pepper

1   Peel carrots and cut into 2 1/2 cm (1 inch) long pieces. Peel and quarter onions. Remove any tough or bruised outer leaves from cabbage. Core, halve, and quarter cabbage.
2   If using food processor, fit with steel blade and process carrots until reduced to small pieces. Remove carrots and coarsely chop cabbage. Remove cabbage, fit processor with slicing disc, and thinly slice carrots. Or, use chef's knife to coarsely chop carrots and cabbage, and to slice onions; set aside.

3 Cut sausage into 5 mm (¹/₄ inch) slices; set aside.
4 In large heavy-gauge non-aluminium saucepan, heat oil over medium-high heat. Add carrots, onions, and sausage, and cook, stirring frequently, until onions are golden, about 3 to 5 minutes. Reduce heat, if necessary, to prevent scorching.
5 While onions are cooking, drain 3 plum tomatoes and reserve remaining tomatoes and liquid for another use. Peel and mince garlic.
6 When onions are golden, tilt pan and spoon off all but about 4 tablespoons fat, if necessary. Stir in cabbage, tomatoes, garlic, bay leaves, and herbs, and cook, stirring frequently, over medium-high heat 3 to 4 minutes, or until aromatic.
7 Meanwhile, bring stock to a simmer in small saucepan over high heat. Turn beans into strainer, rinse under cold running water, and drain. Reduce heat under stock and keep hot.
8 Add wine and rice to vegetable-sausage mixture and bring to a boil, stirring to prevent rice from sticking.
9 Reduce heat under rice to medium, stir in 500 ml (1 pt) hot stock, cover pan, and cook, stirring occasionally to prevent sticking, about 10 minutes, or until stock is absorbed and mixture is creamy.
10 Add beans and 500 ml (1 pt) more hot stock to rice and cook, stirring occasionally, another 10 minutes, or until rice is *al dente* and consistency is quite creamy.
11 Remove risotto from heat, cover pan, and set aside to rest for about 15 minutes.

12 Preheat oven to SLOW and place heatproof serving bowl in oven to warm.
13 If after resting rice still tastes raw, add more stock, cover, and cook another few minutes until stock is absorbed.
14 Remove bay leaves and rosemary sprig, add salt and pepper to taste, and turn into warm serving bowl.

Added touch
These hazelnut meringues, a Piedmontese speciality known as bruti ma buoni ('ugly but good'), are an excellent dessert served with espresso.

Hazelnut Meringues

350 g (12 oz) shelled hazelnuts
175 g (6 oz) sugar
¹/₂ teaspoon cinnamon
4 egg whites, at room temperature
2 teaspoons unsalted butter
2 tablespoons plain flour, approximately

1 Preheat oven to 180°C (350°F or Mark 4).
2 Arrange nuts in single layer on large baking sheet and place in oven. Toast nuts, shaking pan occasionally to prevent nuts from scorching, 15 to 20 minutes, or until skins have split open and meat is light golden brown.
3 Remove nuts from oven and set aside. Reduce oven temperature to 130°C (250°F or Mark ¹/₂).
4 Remove skins from nuts by rubbing with clean kitchen towel. Transfer half of the nuts to food processor fitted with steel blade and chop coarsely. Turn chopped nuts into medium-size bowl. Process remaining nuts to a paste.
5 Add sugar, cinnamon, and nut paste to chopped nuts, and stir to combine.
6 In large copper or stainless-steel bowl, beat egg whites with electric beater at high speed, or with whisk, until soft peaks form.
7 Add nut mixture to egg whites and fold in until incorporated. Don't worry about the whites deflating.
8 Butter and flour a large cookie sheet; shake off excess flour.
9 Drop about 30 teaspoons batter onto sheet, spacing them about 2¹/₂ cm (1 inch) apart. Bake 1 hour to 1 hour and 10 minutes, or until firm and dry. When done, turn off oven but do *not* open oven door again.
10 Allow meringues to rest in oven 1 hour, then remove from oven, and cool to room temperature.

Renaissance Almond Broth
Sweet and Savoury Grilled Lamb
Herb-Roasted Potatoes

Bowls of almond broth precede the entrée of sliced lamb and roast potatoes garnished with fresh parsley.

Grilled butterflied leg of lamb flavoured with a butter that contains crushed juniper berries is an elegant main dish for a special dinner party. The meat of a butterflied leg has been carefully cut off the bone in one large piece so that it resembles a butterfly when laid out. Some sections of the butterflied leg will be thicker than others and will cook more slowly. Test for doneness in the thickest portion. Allow the lamb to rest for 15 minutes while you serve the soup.

Juniper berries, the dried blue fruit of small evergreen shrubs, are available in the spice section of most supermarkets. If you wish to intensify their bittersweet flavour, toast the berries lightly in a dry skillet for a minute or two, then crush them before adding them to the lamb filling.

Balsamic vinegar is a primary flavouring for the roast potatoes. Produced in the Modena province of the Emilia-Romagna region, this unique vinegar has a rich but not cloying flavour with woody and herbal overtones. It is delicious on salads and vegetables. Italian markets and speciality food shops sell this quality vinegar.

What to drink
A dry, fruity red wine suits this menu. The first choice would be a Dolcetto; good alternatives are a French Beaujolais or a California Gamay.

Start-to-Finish Steps

Thirty minutes ahead: Place chicken in freezer to chill.

1 Prepare fresh herbs, if using.
2 Follow potatoes recipe steps 1 through 4.
3 Follow lamb recipe steps 1 through 3.
4 Follow soup recipe steps 1 through 3.
5 Follow lamb recipe step 4.
6 Follow potatoes recipe step 5 and lamb recipe step 5; potatoes will roast while lamb grills.
7 Follow soup recipe steps 4 and 5, and lamb recipe step 6.
8 Follow soup recipe step 6.
9 Follow lamb recipe step 7 and potatoes recipe step 6.
10 Follow soup recipe step 7 and serve.
11 Follow lamb recipe step 8 and potatoes recipe step 7 and serve together.

Renaissance Almond Broth

1 ltr (1³/₄ pts) homemade chicken stock
Small clove garlic
125 g (4 oz) blanched slivered almonds
Pinch of cinnamon
Small bunch fresh chives or scallions

60–100 g (2–3 oz) skinless, boneless chicken breast half, well chilled
Salt and freshly ground black pepper

1 In medium-size heavy-gauge non-aluminium saucepan, bring stock to a boil over medium-high heat.
2 Peel garlic and process with almonds and cinnamon in processor or blender until almonds are powdered.
3 As soon as stock comes to a boil, add almond mixture, cover pan, and remove from heat. Let soup steep, covered, about 30 minutes.
4 Wash and dry chives or scallions. Cut enough chives or scallion greens into 2¹/₂ cm (1 inch) lengths to measure 2 tablespoons and set aside; reserve remainder for another use.
5 About 10 minutes before serving, remove chicken from freezer. With very sharp carving knife, shave chicken into paper-thin slices, moving knife across the grain and away from you. Arrange slices in single layer on large flat plate and season with salt and pepper to taste.
6 About 5 minutes before serving, strain broth through a fine sieve or strainer set over a medium-size bowl, pressing solids with back of spoon to extract as much liquid as possible. Return soup to saucepan and bring to a simmer over medium heat. Adjust seasoning.
7 Just before serving, add chicken slices to soup (they will cook in soup) and immediately ladle into 4 small bowls. Garnish with chopped chives or scallions and serve.

Sweet and Savoury Grilled Lamb

2 large cloves garlic
Large orange
6 juniper berries
4 tablespoons unsalted butter
2 tablespoons dry vermouth
¹/₄ teaspoon chopped fresh rosemary, or ¹/₄ teaspoon dried, plus 4 sprigs for garnish (optional)
¹/₄ teaspoon ground cloves
¹/₂ teaspoon freshly ground black pepper
Pinch of salt
3 large shallots
1.5 Kg (3 lb) loin half of leg of lamb, boned, butterflied, and trimmed

1 Peel and mince garlic. With zester, grate orange rind, reserving orange for another use. Crush juniper berries by placing them under flat blade of chef's knife and hitting blade sharply with heel of hand.

2 Combine all ingredients except shallots and lamb in small heavy-gauge non-aluminium saucepan and bring to a boil over medium heat. Reduce heat and simmer 2 minutes.

3 While butter-spice blend is simmering, peel and finely chop shallots. Stir shallots into butter, remove pan from heat, and allow to cool.

4 Place lamb on rack in grill pan. Using sharp paring knife, make about twelve 2½–3½ cm (1–1½ inch) incisions at an angle, randomly spaced in surface of meat. Using a teaspoon, stuff incisions with butter mixture. Set lamb aside at room temperature.

5 Adjust grill pan so that lamb is about 10 cm (6 inches) from heating element, and grill 10 minutes.

6 For rare lamb, turn and grill another 5 minutes. For medium, grill another 2 to 3 minutes.

7 Turn off grill, leave oven door ajar, and let lamb rest about 15 minutes.

8 To serve, thinly slice lamb across grain. Divide slices among dinner plates and garnish each serving with a sprig of rosemary, if desired.

Herb-Roasted Potatoes

1 Kg (2 lb) small red-skinned new potatoes
8 leaves fresh sage, or 1 teaspoon dried
Salt and freshly ground black pepper
5 tablespoons extra-virgin olive oil
4 tablespoons balsamic vinegar
12 sprigs fresh parsley for garnish (optional)

1 Preheat oven to 220°C (425°F or Mark 7).
2 Wash potatoes thoroughly under cold running water but do not peel; dry with paper towels.

3 Place potatoes in roasting pan, sprinkle with whole sage leaves and salt and pepper to taste, and drizzle with olive oil. Toss potatoes until evenly coated with oil and seasonings.

4 Place pan on lower oven rack and roast 25 minutes, turning occasionally to prevent sticking.

5 Remove potatoes from oven and turn on broiler. Sprinkle potatoes with 3 tablespoons vinegar and return to oven to continue roasting 15 to 20 minutes.

6 Remove potatoes from oven and cover loosely with foil to keep warm until ready to serve.

7 Use slotted spoon to divide potatoes among dinner plates; sprinkle with remaining vinegar and garnish each serving with parsley sprigs, if desired.

Baked Courgettes and Tomatoes

3 medium-size courgettes (about 625 g (1¼ lb) total weight)
6 plum or other small vine-ripened tomatoes (about 625 g (1¼ lb) total weight)
4 tablespoons extra-virgin olive oil
Salt and freshly ground black pepper
30 g (1 oz) parsley sprigs
1 tablespoon chopped fresh basil, or 1 teaspoon dried
2 teaspoons fresh marjoram leaves, or ½ teaspoon dried
Small clove garlic, peeled
½ small onion
1 cm (½ inch) thick slice stale Italian or French bread
1 tablespoon unsalted butter

1 Preheat oven to 200°C (400°F or Mark 6).
2 Wash courgettes and tomatoes, and dry with paper towels. Trim off ends from courgettes and discard. Cut courgettes on diagonal into 5 mm (¼ inch) thick slices. Core tomatoes and cut into thin wedges.

3 Coat bottom and sides of medium-size heavy-gauge baking dish with 1 tablespoon olive oil. Arrange alternating slices of courgettes and tomatoes in rows, reversing slant of slices so that adjacent rows slant in opposite directions. Sprinkle with salt and pepper to taste and drizzle with 1 teaspoon olive oil.

4 Combine parsley, basil, marjoram, garlic, onion, bread, and butter in food processor or blender and process until finely minced. Do *not* overprocess. Season mixture to taste with salt and pepper.

5 Spread mixture over vegetables and drizzle with remaining olive oil. Bake about 45 minutes, or until courgettes can be pierced easily with tip of knife.

<table>
<tr><td>Menu
3</td><td>**Prosciutto and Mostarda di Cremona**
Minestrone with Chickpeas</td></tr>
</table>

For a quick supper, offer prosciutto with mostarda di Cremona *and then bowls of hearty minestrone with crusty bread.*

29

The elegant appetizer for this easy menu pairs delicate prosciutto with the spicy-sweet fruits of *mostarda di Cremona*. Sold in jars at speciality food shops, these fruits preserved in syrup are flavoured with yellow mustard seeds, spices, and sometimes mustard oil. Refrigerate them after opening, and eat them within a month. If *mostarda di Cremona* is unavailable, use whole fresh ripe figs or sweet pears instead.

Both dried Greek oregano and dried *porcini* mushrooms add flavour to the main-course soup. Greek oregano is milder and sweeter than the more commonly sold Mexican variety. Check the label for country of origin. Dried *porcini* mushrooms have a powerful flavour. Select those that are light coloured and not too crumbly; they store well for up to two years.

What to drink
To complement this hearty country fare, choose a rustic red wine such as a Sangiovese di Romagna or a red Lacryma Christi.

Start-to-Finish Steps
1 Follow minestrone recipe steps 1 through 6.
2 While vegetables are cooking, follow prosciutto recipe steps 1 through 3.
3 Follow minestrone recipe steps 7 through 12.
4 While pasta is cooking, follow prosciutto recipe steps 4 and 5.
5 Follow minestrone recipe step 13, prosciutto recipe step 6, if using pears, and serve prosciutto and fruits as first course.
6 Follow minestrone recipe step 14 and serve.

Prosciutto and Mostarda di Cremona

Small head lettuce
12 thin slices prosciutto (about 125 g (4 oz))
125 g (4 oz) candied mustard fruits, such as mostarda di Cremona, or 4 fresh ripe figs or 4 ripe Bartlett pears
1 lemon or lime (optional), plus additional lemon if using pears

1 Rinse lettuce and dry in salad spinner or with paper towels. Discard any blemished outer leaves. Reserve 4 leaves and refrigerate remainder for another use.
2 Roll each slice of prosciutto into a large cone. Arrange 3 cones on each serving plate, with points together in fan-like shape.
3 If using mustard fruits, select whole fruits in contrasting colours, such as a fig, apricot, or small pear; cut larger fruits into quarters. If using figs, peel carefully. If using pears, combine juice of 1 lemon and 1¼ ltrs (2 pts) cold water in large bowl. Peel pears, placing each in bowl as you finish peeling to prevent discolouration.
4 Place a lettuce leaf at the point of each prosciutto fan and top leaf with some mustard fruits, or with a whole peeled fig.
5 If mustard fruits are too sweet, halve lemon or lime and squeeze a little juice over each serving. Cover plates loosely with plastic wrap and set in cool place until ready to serve. Do not refrigerate.
6 If using pears, just before serving, drain and divide among plates.

Minestrone with Chickpeas

25 g (³/₄ oz) dried porcini mushrooms or cèpes
Small bunch fresh parsley
1 stalk celery with leaves
Small bunch fresh basil, or 2 teaspoons dried
Medium-size carrot
3 medium-size onions (about 500 g (1 lb) total weight)
2 large cloves garlic
1 pork loin chop (about 175 g (6 oz))
250 g (8 oz) smoked country-style bacon, sliced
3 tablespoons extra-virgin olive oil
175 g (6 oz) Parmesan cheese, preferably imported
³/₄ teaspoon dried oregano, preferably Greek
500 g (1 lb) canned chickpeas
300 g (10 oz) tomato purée
500 g (1 lb) canned Italian plum tomatoes
Medium-size courgette
175 g (6 oz) pickled sweet red peppers
1¹/₂ ltrs (2¹/₂ pts) homemade chicken stock
175 g (6 oz) pappardelle or other dry, flat, broad pasta
Salt and freshly ground black pepper

1 In small bowl, combine dried mushrooms with enough hot water to cover and set aside for at least 15 minutes.
2 Wash parsley, celery, and fresh basil, if using, and dry with paper towels. Reserve 15 g (¹/₂ oz) parsley; refrigerate remainder for another use. Chop enough basil to measure 2 tablespoons. Trim celery and cut into large pieces. Trim and peel carrot; cut into large pieces. Peel onions. Peel and mince garlic.
3 Remove bone from pork chop and discard; coarsely chop meat. Coarsely chop bacon.
4 Heat oil in large heavy-gauge non-aluminium saucepan or casserole over medium-high heat. Add bacon and chopped pork, and sauté, stirring frequently, 5 to 7 minutes or until golden.
5 Meanwhile, if using food processor, grate enough cheese to measure 175 g (6 oz) and transfer to small serving bowl. Or, using grater, grate cheese. Add celery and carrot, and process until medium-fine. With slicing disc, slice onions over vegetables. If using chef's knife, finely chop parsley, celery, and carrot, and thinly slice onions.
6 When meat is done, carefully spoon off all but 3 tablespoons of fat. Add vegetables, stirring to scrape up any brown bits clinging to bottom of pan. Cover, reduce heat to medium-low, and cook 10 minutes.
7 Add mushrooms and, using fine sieve or strainer lined with paper towel, strain soaking liquid into pan. Stir in minced garlic and herbs, and simmer gently 2 to 3 minutes, or until aromatic.
8 Meanwhile, turn chickpeas into sieve or strainer, rinse under cold running water, and drain; set aside.
9 Add tomato purée and plum tomatoes with their liquid to pan, bring to the boil, stirring, and simmer briskly 5 minutes.
10 Wash courgettes and dry. Trim off ends and discard; cut courgettes into 1 cm (¹/₂ inch) dice. Drain red peppers and rinse under cold running water. Pat dry with paper towels and cut into 5 mm (¹/₄ inch) wide strips.
11 Add chickpeas, courgettes, and red pepper strips to pan, and cook, stirring, 1 minute.
12 Stir in chicken stock and bring to a simmer. Add pasta and cook, stirring frequently, 6 to 8 minutes, or until pasta is tender but not mushy.
13 Season with salt and pepper to taste and remove pan from heat. Cover and allow to rest about 10 minutes.
14 If necessary, reheat soup briefly over medium heat before serving. To serve, divide among soup bowls, garnish each with a generous spoonful of Parmesan, and offer remaining cheese separately.

Susan DeRege

Menu 1
(*left*)
Piedmontese Pork Medallions
Straw and Hay Pasta with Butter Sauce
Carrots with Kirsch

Susan DeRege spends long hours in the kitchen almost daily as part of her job, yet she never tires of cooking at home for friends and family. She likes meals that can be prepared ahead, allowing her to spend time with her guests. The three menus she presents here are all based on the cooking of northern Italy.

The pork medallions and the glazed carrots in Menu 1, both Piedmont recipes, can be prepared early in the day, refrigerated, and then quickly reheated for the table. The straw and hay pasta – a recipe from Emilia-Romagna – should be prepared just before dinner.

Menu 3 is a favourite of this cook because it can be made a day ahead and is perfect for either a buffet or a sit-down dinner. The Ligurian artichoke soup is equally good chilled or heated, and the peppers can be served at room temperature or hot. The veal entrée, a Piedmont dish, is named for Count Cavour, the nineteenth-century statesman who came from the region.

Menu 2 is a bit more complicated. The creamy risotto requires constant stirring, so Susan DeRege suggests inviting your guests into the kitchen for a glass of wine while you prepare the meal. The risotto is bound with Parmesan cheese, which also flavours the accompanying Milanese-style chicken. In an Italian home, the endive salad would be served after the main course

Casual pottery underscores the simplicity of this family meal: pork medallions with a sweet and sour sauce and finger carrots glazed with fruity kirsch. The two-toned pasta dish, tossed with butter, is sprinkled with freshly grated Parmesan and black pepper.

Piedmontese Pork Medallions
Straw and Hay Pasta with Butter Sauce
Carrots with Kirsch

The yellow and green egg noodles may be served as the appetizer or as an accompaniment to the pork medallions and carrots. If the cooked pasta is too dry after adding the Parmesan, tossing the pasta with a little of the hot cooking water will improve the sauce.

The pork medallions simmer gently in milk flavoured with rosemary and vinegar. Soft curds may appear when you first add the vinegar to the milk, but after slow cooking they will almost disappear. If you want an especially smooth sauce, blend the milk mixture in your blender or food processor for a few seconds.

What to drink

A dry but not overpowering red wine, such as a Spanna or a Nebbiolo from the Italian Piedmont, would make the best partner for these dishes.

Start-to-Finish Steps

1 Follow pork recipe steps 1 through 3 and carrots recipe steps 1 and 2.
2 Follow pasta recipe steps 1 and 2.
3 Follow carrots recipe steps 3 and 4.
4 Follow pasta recipe steps 3 through 7.
5 Follow pork recipe step 4 and serve with pasta and carrots.

Piedmontese Pork Medallions

1 tablespoon virgin olive oil
1 tablespoon unsalted butter
750 g (1½ lb) boneless pork loin roast from the rib end, cut into 12 medallions and pounded 1 cm (½ inch) thick
Salt and freshly ground black pepper
350 ml (12 fl oz) milk
3 tablespoons balsamic vinegar
3 sprigs fresh rosemary, or 1½ teaspoons dried rosemary, crushed, plus 4 sprigs for garnish (optional)

1 Heat olive oil and butter in large heavy-gauge skillet over high heat. Place about half the medallions in skillet in a single layer and sauté about 3 minutes per side, or until brown. As they brown, transfer

medallions to platter and season with salt and pepper to taste. Repeat process for remaining medallions.

2 Lower heat under skillet to medium-high. Add milk slowly to prevent boiling, stirring and scraping up any browned bits clinging to bottom of pan. Stir in vinegar and rosemary. Cover pan and bring liquid to a boil.

3 When liquid comes to a boil, reduce heat to low. Return all the medallions to skillet, cover partially, and cook, turning occasionally with tongs, 25 to 35 minutes, or until pork is fork-tender and sauce is caramel coloured and has reduced to 125 ml (4 fl oz).

4 Remove rosemary sprigs and discard. Divide medallions among plates and top each serving with sauce. Garnish each plate with a sprig of fresh rosemary, if desired.

Straw and Hay Pasta with Butter Sauce

60 g (2 oz) unsalted butter
1½ tablespoons salt
175 g (6 oz) green fettuccine plus 175 g (6 oz) white
125 g (4 oz) Parmesan cheese
Freshly ground black pepper

1 Bring 6 ltrs (10 pts) cold water to a boil over high heat in stockpot or large kettle. Preheat oven to SLOW and place 4 bowls in oven to warm.

2 While water is coming to a boil, cut butter into 8 pieces, transfer to large ovenproof bowl or casserole, and place in oven.

3 Add salt and pasta to boiling water and stir with wooden spoon to blend green and white noodles. Cook pasta 8 to 12 minutes, or just until *al dente*.

4 In food processor or with grater, grate enough Parmesan to measure 100 g (3 oz); set aside.

5 When pasta is almost cooked, remove 60 ml (2 fl oz) pasta water and reserve. Turn pasta into colander and drain.

6 Transfer pasta to bowl with melted butter and toss until well coated. Add pepper and 60 g (2 oz) Parmesan, and toss again. If pasta is still too dry,

add a little reserved pasta water and toss to combine.

7 Divide pasta among warm bowls, sprinkle each serving with Parmesan, and add a few twists of black pepper; serve remaining cheese separately.

Carrots with Kirsch

14–16 medium carrots, about 1.25 Kg (2^1/$_2$ lb) total weight
Small bunch fresh parsley
6 tablespoons butter
^{1}/$_2$ teaspoon salt
Freshly ground black pepper
^{1}/$_4$ cup kirsch

1 Trim and peel carrots. If using finger carrots, leave whole, or halve regular carrots lengthwise, cut crosswise into 5 cm (2 inch) pieces, then cut into 1 cm (^{1}/$_2$ inch) julienne. Wash parsley, dry, and chop enough to measure 2 tablespoons; set aside.

2 In medium-size skillet, bring 1 cm (^{1}/$_2$ inch) water to a boil over medium-high heat. Add carrots, cover, and cook 6 to 8 minutes, or until they are crisp-tender. Be careful not to let water boil away or carrots will burn.

3 Pour off any water remaining in skillet and lower heat to medium. Add butter, salt, pepper to taste, and kirsch; cook, shaking pan to dissipate alcohol, 3 to 4 minutes, or until carrots are glazed.

4 Turn carrots into medium-size ovenproof bowl, sprinkle with chopped parsley, and keep warm in SLOW oven until ready to serve.

Added touch

For this elegant dessert, ripe pears are served in a *zabaglione*, a foamy custard, and drizzled with melted semi-sweet chocolate.

Pears Contessa

4 egg yolks
125 g (4 oz) sugar
125 ml (4 fl oz) dry Marsala
Juice of 1 lemon
4 ripe pears with stems intact
125 ml (4 fl oz) heavy cream
60 g (2 oz) imported semi-sweet chocolate

1 Place medium-size bowl and beaters in freezer to chill.

2 Combine egg yolks and sugar in small heavy-gauge non-aluminium saucepan and whisk until thick and fluffy. Gradually add Marsala, whisking until blended.

3 Place saucepan over medium heat and whisk egg mixture briskly until it coats whisk and mounds slightly, about 7 minutes.

4 Turn zabaglione into stainless-steel mixing bowl, cover with plastic wrap, and place in freezer to chill, about 25 minutes.

5 Meanwhile, combine lemon juice and 1^1/$_4$ ltrs (2 pts) cold water in large mixing bowl. Peel pears, placing each in lemon water as you finish peeling it to prevent discolouration.

6 In chilled bowl, beat heavy cream with electric mixer at high speed until stiff. Fold about 60 ml (2 fl oz) of chilled zabaglione into the whipped cream, then fold in remaining zabaglione.

7 Pour zabaglione cream into centre of gently sloping bowl or 2 ltr (3 pt) soufflé dish. Arrange whole pears around edge, cover with plastic wrap, and refrigerate until ready to serve.

8 Just before serving, melt chocolate in top of double boiler over hot, not boiling, water.

9 Drizzle melted chocolate over pears and zabaglione, and divide among individual plates.

Chicken Breasts Milanese
Risotto with Porcini Mushrooms
Endive salad with Green Herb Sauce

Instead of using the traditional – and expensive – veal cutlets for this entrée, the cook prepares chicken breasts. However, you can use turkey breasts instead. Dipping the breasts into the seasoned beaten-egg mixture before coating them helps the bread crumbs and Parmesan adhere to the meat.

A good risotto requires patience – here you stir the rice continuously while slowly adding the broth. The trick is not to overcook the dense, creamy mixture because the risotto continues cooking even when removed from the heat.

The endive salad is dressed with a piquant green sauce *(bagnetto verde)*. The sauce is quickly prepared in a food processor or blender and keeps well in the refrigerator for up to a month.

What to drink

This menu deserves either a full-bodied white wine or a light-bodied red. For white, the cook suggests Fiano di Avellino; for red, Grignolino.

Start-to-Finish Steps

1 Prepare parsley, watercress, and fresh herbs, if using. Grate enough Parmesan to measure 1 cup and set aside.
2 Follow risotto recipe steps 1 and 2 and chicken recipe steps 1 through 3.
3 Follow salad recipe steps 1 through 3.
4 Follow herb sauce recipe steps 1 through 3.
5 Follow chicken recipe steps 4 through 6.
6 Follow risotto recipe steps 3 through 7.
7 Follow salad recipe step 4, chicken recipe step 7, and serve with risotto.

Chicken Breasts Milanese

1 lemon
2 eggs
60 g (2 oz) freshly grated Parmesan cheese
Salt and freshly ground black pepper

Crumb-coated chicken breasts, risotto with porcini mushrooms, and an endive salad are a classic northern Italian meal.

2 skinless, boneless chicken breasts (about 750 g
      (1½ lb) total weight), halved and trimmed
60 g (2 oz) dry white bread crumbs
3 tablespoons unsalted butter
4 tablespoons corn oil
1 sprig fresh rosemary, or ½ teaspoon dried
4 sprigs parsley for garnish (optional)

1   Rinse lemon and dry. Cut into 4 wedges and set
    aside.
2   In medium-size bowl, combine eggs, 30 g (1 oz)
    of the Parmesan, and salt and pepper to taste, and
    beat until well blended. Add chicken breasts to
    egg mixture, turn to coat, and set aside to soak
    about 10 minutes.
3   Combine remaining cheese and bread crumbs in
    pie pan; set aside.
4   Preheat oven to SLOW. Line heatproof serving
    platter with paper towels.
5   In large heavy-gauge skillet, heat butter, corn oil,
    and rosemary over medium-high heat.
6   While fat is heating, dredge each chicken piece in
    crumb-cheese mixture until evenly coated. When
    butter stops foaming, add chicken to pan and
    sauté 4 to 5 minutes per side, or until golden
    brown. Transfer to paper-towel-lined platter and
    keep warm in oven until ready to serve.
7   Remove paper towels from platter and garnish
    chicken with lemon wedges and parsley sprigs, if
    desired.

Risotto with Porcini Mushrooms

15 g (½ oz) dried porcini mushrooms
Small yellow onion
750 ml (1½ pts) combined chicken and beef stock
4 tablespoons unsalted butter
1 tablespoon corn oil
Pinch of dried rosemary
300 g (10 oz) Italian Arborio rice
2 tablespoons dry sherry
¼ teaspoon salt
60 g (2 oz) freshly grated Parmesan cheese

1   Rinse mushrooms under cold water. Place them in
    small bowl, cover with warm water, and soak 20
    minutes.
2   Peel and finely chop enough onion to measure 2
    tablespoons; set aside.
3   Place serving bowl in SLOW oven. Bring stock to
    a boil in medium-size saucepan over high heat,
    then reduce heat to just maintain a simmer.

4   While stock is heating, combine 3 tablespoons
    butter, oil, rosemary, and onion in large heavy-
    gauge saucepan or enamel-lined casserole over
    medium heat and sauté, stirring occasionally, 5 to
    8 minutes, or just until onions are translucent. Add
    rice and stir until translucent and well coated with
    fat; do not brown.
5   Lower heat slightly and add hot stock gradually,
    about 125 ml (4 fl oz) at a time, stirring constantly
    after each addition until stock is totally absorbed
    by rice. Add mushrooms and their soaking liquid
    to rice. Add sherry and continue stirring over
    medium-low heat until liquid is absorbed, about
    20 minutes.
6   When liquid is absorbed, stir in salt and 30 g (1 oz)
    Parmesan.
7   Remove pan from heat and stir in remaining
    tablespoon butter. Turn risotto into warm serving
    bowl and offer remaining cheese separately.

Endive salad with Green Herb Sauce

2 medium-size heads Belgian endive (about 250 g
      (8 oz) total weight)
Medium-size carrot
8 sprigs watercress
Green Herb Sauce (see following recipe)

1   Halve, core, and separate endive leaves. Wash
    thoroughly and dry with paper towels.

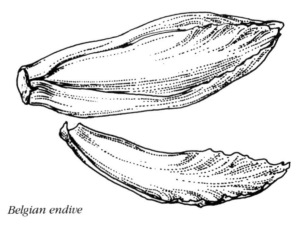

Belgian endive

2   Trim and peel carrot. Halve carrot lengthwise and
    cut halves into 5 cm (2 inch) pieces. Cut each piece
    into thin matchsticks.
3   Divide endive among individual salad plates and
    top with watercress. Sprinkle each serving with

carrot sticks, cover with plastic wrap, and refrigerate until ready to serve.

4 Just before serving, remove salads from refrigerator and place a generous spoonful of green herb sauce on each plate.

Green Herb Sauce

1 sprig fresh rosemary, or 1½ teaspoons dried
1 tablespoon capers
60 g (2 oz) fresh parsley
3 leaves fresh sage, or ½ teaspoon dried
2 leaves fresh basil, or ¼ teaspoon dried
1 teaspoon dried thyme
1 teaspoon dried oregano
¼ teaspoon chili powder
1 very large clove garlic
¼ teaspoon salt
¼ teaspoon freshly ground pepper
1 tablespoon red wine vinegar
4 tablespoons virgin olive oil
2 anchovies
4 tablespoons tomato sauce

1 Strip leaves from rosemary. Drain capers in small strainer and rinse under cold running water.
2 In food processor or blender, process all ingredients, except olive oil, anchovies, and tomato sauce, until finely chopped.
3 Add remaining ingredients and purée. Adjust seasoning and set aside at room temperature until ready to serve.

Added touch

For this version of the traditional Italian custard called *panna cotta*, or cooked cream, use a brioche pan to mould the dessert. This classic pan has fluted sides that flare outward from a small round base. Oil the pan before adding the hot custard to make unmoulding easier. If you do not have a brioche pan, a 1¼ ltr (2 pt) soufflé dish or glass baking dish works well.

Moulded Caramel Custard

60 ml (2 fl oz) milk
125 g (4 oz) plus 3 tablespoons sugar
2 teaspoons unflavoured gelatin
4 egg yolks
Pinch of Salt
2 tablespoons praline liqueur or Cognac
350 ml (12 fl oz) heavy cream

1 Place bowl and beaters for whipping cream in freezer to chill.
2 In small heavy-gauge non-aluminium saucepan, heat milk over medium heat just until it begins to boil. Remove pan from heat.
3 In tea kettle or small saucepan, bring about 250 ml (8 fl oz) water to a boil.
4 In small heavy-gauge sauté pan, melt 125 g (4 oz) sugar over low heat, stirring constantly, 8 to 10 minutes, or until melted and straw coloured.
5 Remove pan from heat and *very* slowly add 2 tablespoons of the boiling water, stirring constantly, until water is incorporated. Return pan to low heat and cook another 5 minutes, or until caramel thickens.
6 Meanwhile, combine gelatin and 2 tablespoons cold water in small bowl and stir until gelatin dissolves.
7 In medium-size heavy-gauge saucepan, combine egg yolks, remaining sugar, and salt. Add a little hot water milk to yolks and stir until melted. Slowly stir in remainder of the milk and cook over low heat, about 5 minutes, or until mixture is thick enough to coat a spoon.
8 Stir in gelatin until incorporated. Stir in two thirds of the warm caramel mixture and the liqueur, cover, and chill in freezer 15 to 20 minutes, or until custard is consistency of stiffly beaten heavy cream.
9 Meanwhile, beat heavy cream until stiff, then gently fold into the chilled custard. Pour into an oiled brioche pan and chill at least 3 hours or overnight.
10 When ready to serve, dip bottom of mould briefly in warm water. Place flat serving plate upside down over pan, tap once sharply against hard surface, and, holding firmly together, invert. Remove pan, drizzle custard with remaining caramel, and serve.

<table>
<tr>
<td>

Menu

<u>**3**</u>
</td>
<td>

Cream of Artichoke Soup
Veal Scallopini Cavour
Peperonata
</td>
</tr>
</table>

For this meal the veal is coated evenly with flour, quickly sautéed, and then braised until tender. This technique allows you to use meat from the rump or lower part of the leg rather than expensive top round. The flour browns to a crust and also helps to thicken the braising liquid as the meat cooks. If you assemble all of the ingredients for the veal dish before heating the fat, you can put the meat right into the pan as you dredge the veal. Do not let the meat sit in the flour or the coating will become soggy and stick to the pan rather than to the meat.

For the Italian-style peppers, buy only red and yellow bell peppers that have a uniform, glossy colour and thick flesh; they should feel firm and heavy.

Refrigerated in a plastic bag, unwashed peppers keep for up to a week.

What to drink

A white Italian Gavi or top-quality Soave, or a red Dolcetto or Chianti Classico, are all good with veal.

Start-to-Finish Steps

One hour ahead: Set out frozen artichoke hearts to thaw for soup recipe.

1 Wash parsley and dry with paper towels. Reserve 4 parsley sprigs for soup garnish, if desired, and chop enough to measure 1 tablespoon for veal

The artichoke soup may be served before the entrée of braised veal and strips of sautéed red and yellow peppers.

recipe; refrigerate remainder for another use. Squeeze enough juice from 1 lemon to measure 3 tablespoons for veal recipe. If using lemon for soup garnish, rinse, dry, and cut remaining lemon crosswise into 8 very thin slices.

2 Follow soup recipe steps 1 through 3.
3 While soup is simmering, follow veal recipe steps 1 through 5 and set pan aside.
4 Follow soup recipe step 4 and peppers recipe steps 1 and 2.
5 Follow soup recipe steps 5 and 6.
6 Follow veal recipe step 6, peppers recipe step 3, and soup recipe step 7.
7 Follow peppers recipe step 4.
8 Follow soup recipe step 8 and serve as first course.

Cream of Artichoke Soup

Small yellow onion
500 g (1 lb) frozen artichoke hearts, thawed
350 ml (12 fl oz) milk
1 teaspoon salt
1 teaspoon sugar
2 eggs
250 ml (8 fl oz) heavy cream
Freshly ground white pepper
8 very thin slices lemon for garnish (optional)
4 parsley sprigs for garnish (optional)

1 Peel and finely chop enough onion to measure 60g (2 oz).
2 Combine artichoke hearts, milk, salt, sugar, and chopped onion in medium-size non-aluminium saucepan, and simmer over medium-high heat 20 minutes. Do *not* boil.
3 Meanwhile, separate eggs into 2 small bowls, reserving whites for another use.
4 After 20 minutes, remove pan from heat and allow mixture to cool slightly.
5 Transfer mixture to food processor or blender and purée.
6 Rinse saucepan, return purée to pan, and reheat 3 minutes over medium heat; reduce heat to low, if necessary, to prevent boiling.
7 Add heavy cream to egg yolks and whisk until blended. Slowly add small amount of hot purée to cream mixture, whisking until incorporated. Then add warmed cream mixture to saucepan and stir until blended. Add freshly ground pepper to taste and heat briefly.
8 Divide soup among individual bowls and garnish each serving with 2 lemon slices and parsley sprig, if desired.

Veal Scallopini Cavour

2 tablespoons virgin olive oil
4 tablespoons unsalted butter
60 g (2 oz) plain flour
Eight 5 mm (¼ inch) thick veal scallops (about 750 g (1½ lb) total weight), pounded 2½ mm (⅛ inch) thick
Salt and freshly ground black pepper
3 tablespoons lemon juice
100 ml (3 fl oz) dry white vermouth
1 tablespoon chopped parsley

1 Preheat oven to SLOW.
2 Combine oil and 3 tablespoons of the butter in large heavy-gauge skillet over medium-high heat.
3 Meanwhile, place flour in pie pan or on plate. Lightly dredge in flour as many scallops as will fit in skillet without crowding; shake off excess flour.
4 When butter stops foaming, add scallops to skillet and sauté about 2 minutes per side, or until browned. Sprinkle with salt and pepper to taste, transfer to platter, and place in oven. Dredge remaining scallops, sauté, and transfer to platter; return to oven.
5 Remove pan from heat and add lemon juice and vermouth, stirring to scrape up any browned bits clinging to bottom of pan.
6 Return scallops and any accumulated juices to pan, cover, and braise over low heat 25 to 30 minutes, or until tender.
7 Transfer scallops to dinner plates. Add chopped parsley and remaining butter to pan and stir until blended. Pour sauce over scallops and serve.

Peperonata

2 large red bell peppers (about 350 g (12 oz) total weight)
2 large yellow bell peppers (about 350 g (12 oz) total weight)
125 ml (4 fl oz) virgin olive oil
Salt and freshly ground black pepper

1 Wash peppers and dry. Core, halve, and remove seeds and membranes. Cut peppers lengthwise into 1 cm ($^1/_2$ inch) thick strips.

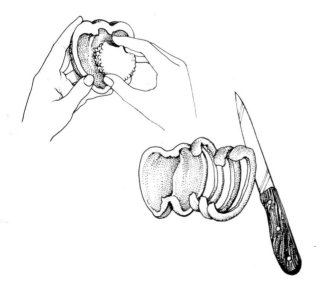

2 Heat olive oil in medium-size skillet over high heat. Add peppers and sauté, stirring, until well coated with oil, 2 to 3 minutes. Cover pan, lower heat to medium, and cook peppers 12 minutes.
3 Remove cover, add salt and pepper to taste, and cook another 10 minutes, or until pan liquid is syrupy.
4 Transfer peppers and syrup to serving dish and keep warm in SLOW oven until ready to serve.

Added touch
For this summertime dessert, use ripe freestone peaches (with easy-to-remove-remove pits) that are firm but yield slightly to pressure. To peel peaches easily, place them in boiling water for 1 minute, then immerse in cold water.

Baked Stuffed Peaches

4 large ripe freestone peaches
125 g (4 oz) granulated sugar
2 tablespoons cocoa powder
30 g (1 oz) blanched almonds, chopped
3 tablespoons grated lemon rind
5 almond macaroons (amaretti), crumbled
1 egg yolk
2 tablespoons Cognac
2 tablespoons unsalted butter

1 Preheat oven to 180°C (350°F or Mark 4).
2 Peel and halve peaches. Remove pits and discard. Using melon baller or teaspoon, scoop out all but 1 cm ($^1/_2$ inch) of pulp. Place pulp in medium-size mixing bowl.
3 To peach pulp, add 60 g (2 oz) sugar, cocoa, almonds, lemon rind, macaroons, egg yolk, and enough Cognac to form a thick paste, and stir to blend.
4 Arrange peach halves in shallow baking dish. Divide filling among halves, dot with butter, and sprinkle with remaining sugar. Bake peaches 20 minutes, or until a slight crust is formed on filling.
5 Divide peaches among individual plates and serve.

Leftover suggestion
Reserve the unused egg whites from the artichoke soup recipe and freeze them until you accumulate enough (about 4 to 6) to make meringues, a popular sweet in Italy. For convenience, put each white into a compartment of an ice cube tray and cover the tray tightly with foil.

Nancy Verde Barr

Menu 1
(*right*)
Braised Duck with Black Olives
Penne with Mushroom Sauce

Nancy Barr is particularly interested in recipes from southern Italy, which was her paternal grandparents' home. As a cooking teacher, her ambition is to familiarize Americans with the diversity of southern Italian food. 'I want people to know that southerners eat so many more dishes than pizza, lasagne, spaghetti, and meatballs!' she says.

Her Menus 1 and 3 introduce easy but relatively unfamiliar southern Italian dishes. In Menu 1, she serves pasta with a highly seasoned tomato sauce from the region of Calabria and couples it with braised duck and black olives from nearby Basilicata. Menu 3 features a courgette soup from Naples, lamb chops cooked with mushrooms (a dish popular in Calabria's province of Catanzaro), and broccoli rabe sautéed with olive oil and garlic.

For a change of pace, in Menu 2 Nancy Barr prepares a simple meal from the region of Abruzzo, where pickled vegetables are often cooked with chicken or veal. The tomatoes are stuffed with a mixture of bread crumbs, capers, anchovies, and *soppressata*, a hard Italian salami.

For this informal dinner, present the pieces of browned duck on a large serving platter, then spoon the olives and other sauce ingredients over the top. Penne in a spicy tomato sauce is a traditional southern Italian partner for duck.

43

Braised Duck with Black Olives
Penne with Mushroom Sauce

Most supermarkets sell frozen whole ducks, but because they are increasingly in demand, you can often find them fresh as well. The skin of fresh ducks should be elastic, free of pinfeathers, and should feel well padded with fat. Keep fresh duck loosely wrapped in the coldest part of the refrigerator for up to three days. Frozen ducks should be securely wrapped in sturdy, unbroken plastic wrap. They can be stored frozen for up to three months. Thaw them in the plastic wrap in the refrigerator 24 to 36 hours before cooking; or, if you are in a hurry, put the frozen duck, still wrapped in waterproof plastic, in a pan of cold water and it will be ready for cooking in about three hours.

The penne, or quill-shaped pasta, is served with a simple sauce sparked with hot pepper flakes. Start with a small amount of flakes, and adjust the seasoning to your taste. If fresh hot chilies are available, try them in place of the pepper flakes. Begin with half a small hot pepper, and increase the amount, if desired. To remove the seeds, wear rubber gloves to protect your hands. The more seeds you leave in, the hotter the flavour.

What to drink
A southern Italian red wine such as the dry and flavourful Taurasi or Aglianico del Vulture complements the strong flavours of the duck.

Start-to-Finish Steps
1 Wash parsley and fresh oregano, if using, and dry with paper towels. Chop enough parsley to measure ½ cup for duck recipe and ¼ cup for pasta recipe; chop enough oregano to measure 2 tablespoons for pasta recipe. Peel and chop onions for duck and pasta recipes.
2 Follow duck recipe steps 1 through 6.
3 While duck is grilling follow pasta recipe steps 1 and 2.
4 Follow duck recipe step 7.
5 While duck is cooking, follow pasta recipe steps 3 through 5.
6 Follow duck recipe steps 8 and 9, and pasta recipe steps 6 through 10.
7 Follow duck recipe step 10 and pasta recipe step 11, and serve together.

Braised Duck with Black Olives

2½ Kg (5 lb) duckling
Small celery stalk
Small carrot
125 g (4 oz) prosciutto, unsliced
125 g (4 oz) pitted black olives
3 tablespoons olive oil
Small onion, peeled and chopped
250 ml (8 fl oz) dry white wine
30 g (1 oz) chopped parsley
1 bay leaf
Salt
Freshly ground black pepper

1 Preheat grill.
2 Remove any excess fat from cavity of duck. Trim off neck skin. Chop off wing tips and reserve with neck

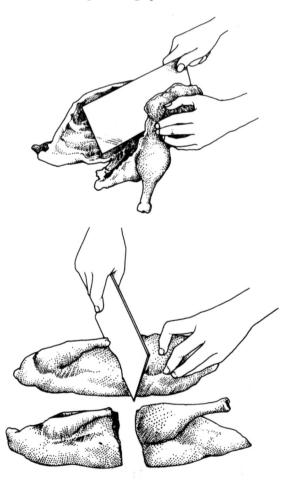

and gizzards for another use. With cleaver, quarter duck: Turn duck skin-side up on cutting surface and cut through the breastbone. Turn duck over, push back breast halves, and cut backbone in two. Next, place each half skin-side up and, feeling for end of rib cage, cut pieces in half just below ribs. Turn quarters skin-side down and, with sharp knife, trim excess skin and any visible fat from each piece.

3   Wash celery, dry, and dice enough to measure 30 g (1 oz). Peel and finely dice enough carrot to measure 30 g (1 oz). Chop prosciutto into 5 mm (¼ inch) dice. Slice olives in half; set aside.

4   Place rack in grill pan. Place duck skin-side up on rack and grill 10 cm (6 inches) away from heating element for 5 minutes.

5   Meanwhile, heat olive oil in large sauté pan over medium heat. Add onion, celery, carrot, and prosciutto and sauté, stirring occasionally, about 10 minutes, or until onion is golden.

6   After duck has grilled 5 minutes, prick skin all over with skewer or tip of paring knife to release fat, being careful not to penetrate meat. Grill another 5 minutes, pricking skin once more during this time. Turn duck and grill another 5 minutes.

7   Transfer duck to sauté pan with vegetables and prosciutto, add wine, and bring to a boil over high heat. Reduce oven temperature to SLOW, leaving door ajar if necessary. Seal pan with sheet of foil, place cover over foil, and cook duck over medium heat 15 minutes.

8   Remove cover and foil, add parsley, bay leaves, olives, and salt and pepper to taste. Reseal pan with foil, re-cover, and cook another 20 minutes, or until tender.

9   Meanwhile, place large heatproof serving platter in oven to warm.

10 When duck is done, transfer to warm platter, top with sauce, and serve.

1   Peel and coarsely chop garlic. Wipe mushrooms clean with damp paper towels and chop coarsely.

2   In strainer set over medium-size bowl, drain tomatoes; reserve juice. Coarsely chop tomatoes; set aside.

3   Heat oil in medium-size sauté pan over medium heat. Add onion and garlic, and sauté, stirring occasionally, 3 to 4 minutes, or until onions are soft and translucent.

4   Raise heat to high, add mushrooms, and salt to taste; sauté 2 to 3 minutes, or until mushrooms exude liquid.

5   Reduce heat to medium. Add tomatoes, 125 ml (4 fl oz) reserved tomato juice, parsley, oregano, red pepper flakes, and salt to taste, and simmer 25 minutes, adding more tomato juice if sauce becomes too thick.

6   Bring 4 ltrs (6 pts) salted water to a boil in stockpot over high heat.

7   Meanwhile, in food processor or with grater, grate enough cheese to make 125 g (4 oz) and set aside.

8   Place large heatproof serving bowl in SLOW oven to warm.

9   Add penne to boiling water and cook according to package directions until *al dente*.

11 Drain pasta in colander.

12 Turn sauce into warm serving bowl, add drained pasta, and toss to combine. Serve with grated cheese.

Penne with Mushroom Sauce

Large clove garlic
350 g (12 oz) mushrooms
1 Kg (2 lb) canned Italian plum tomatoes
3 tablespoons olive oil
Small onion, peeled and chopped
salt
15 g (½ oz) chopped parsley
2 tablespoons chopped fresh oregano, or 2 teaspoons dried
¼ teaspoon red pepper flakes, approximately
125 g (4 oz) pecorino Romano or Parmesan cheese
350 g (12 oz) penne or similarly shaped pasta

Piquant Chicken
Baked Stuffed Tomatoes

For the chicken main dish, the cook suggests butterflying a whole fryer: splitting the bird in half, removing the backbone, and opening the chicken flat. Cooking the chicken this way makes it juicier. Or, have your butcher butterfly the chicken, or substitute a cut-up fryer.

What to drink
A white Lacryma Christi or a top-quality Orvieto would be fine here, or try a California Sauvignon Blanc.

The aromas of the piquant chicken enhance this meal. Spoon some of the sauce with pickled sweet peppers and artichoke hearts over the chicken quarters, and offer a whole baked tomato with each helping.

Start-to-Finish Steps

One hour ahead: Set out artichoke hearts to thaw for chicken recipe.

1 Follow tomatoes recipe steps 1 and 2.
2 Follow chicken recipe steps 1 through 6.
3 While chicken is cooking, follow tomatoes recipe step 3.
4 Follow chicken recipe step 7 and tomatoes recipe steps 4 through 6.
5 Follow chicken recipe step 8 and tomatoes recipe steps 7 and 8.
6 Follow chicken recipe steps 9 through 12, and serve with tomatoes.

Piquant Chicken

1 frying chicken (about 1.5 Kg (3 lb))
2 large cloves garlic
4 tablespoons olive oil
125 g (4 oz) Italian pickled sweet peppers, without liquid
125 ml (4 fl oz) dry white wine
250 g (8 oz) frozen artichoke hearts, thawed
Salt

1 Rinse chicken under cold water and dry with paper towels. To butterfly chicken: Place chicken on cutting surface, breast-side down, with legs pointing toward you. Using poultry shears or chef's knife, cut along each side of backbone as close to the bone as possible. Remove backbone and discard. Turn bird breast-side up and flatten by striking breastbone with the heel of your hand. Cut off wing tips and tuck wings under.

2 Bruise garlic by placing cloves under flat blade of chef's knife; peel.

3 Heat olive oil in large skillet over medium-low heat. Add garlic and sauté, stirring occasionally, 4 to 6 minutes, or until golden. Discard garlic.

4 Place chicken skin-side down in skillet. Raise heat to medium-high and cook about 8 minutes, or until chicken skin is nicely browned.

5 Meanwhile, cut peppers into 1 cm (1/2 inch) by 5 cm (2 inch) long strips; set aside.

6 Turn chicken skin-side up and cook another 7 minutes.

7 Pour off all but 1 tablespoon fat from skillet. Add wine and bring to a boil over high heat; boil 15 seconds. Reduce heat to medium, cover, and cook 15 minutes.

8 Add pepper strips, artichoke hearts, and salt to taste to skillet. Cover and cook another 15 to 20 minutes, or until juices run clear when chicken is pierced with a sharp knife.

9 Toward end of cooking time, place 4 dinner plates under hot running water to warm.

10 When chicken is cooked, remove from pan to cutting surface. With poultry shears or chef's knife,

cut chicken into quarters. Dry plates and transfer chicken pieces to them.

11 Raise heat under skillet to high and boil pan juices, stirring to scrape up any browned bits clinging to bottom of pan, until juices are slightly thickened and glossy, 2 to 4 minutes. There should be about 60 ml (2 fl oz) of pan juices.

12 Top each serving of chicken with a spoonful of pan juices and some vegetables.

Baked Stuffed Tomatoes

4 medium-size tomatoes (about 750 g (1½ lb) total weight)
Salt
3 slices stale bread, approximately
Small bunch parsley
125 g (4 oz) jar capers
2 to 4 anchovy fillets
125 g (4 oz) soppressata or other hard salami
3 tablespoons olive oil, approximately
Freshly ground black pepper

1 Preheat oven to 190°C (375°F or Mark 5).
2 Cut 1 cm (½ inch) slice from tops of tomatoes. Turn each tomato upside down and squeeze gently to remove seeds and juice. Using serrated or regular teaspoon, remove any remaining seeds and enough pulp to make room for stuffing. Sprinkle insides of tomatoes lightly with salt and place upside down on paper-towel-covered cake rack to drain.
3 Trim off crusts from bread and discard. Using food processor or grater, grate enough bread to measure 60 g (2 oz) crumbs.
4 Rinse parsley and dry with paper towels; finely chop enough to measure 15 g (½ oz). Drain 1 tablespoon capers in small strainer and rinse under cold running water; chop finely. Drain anchovies; chop finely. Finely chop soppressata.
5 Combine parsley, capers, anchovies, soppressata, and bread crumbs in small bowl. Add 1 tablespoon olive oil to mixture and stir until blended. Add pepper to taste but *no* salt; the capers and anchovies provide sufficient saltiness.
6 Divide stuffing among tomato shells.
7 Lightly grease shallow baking dish with some of the remaining oil. Place tomatoes upright in dish and drizzle with 1 or 2 teaspoons olive oil.
8 Bake 20 minutes, or until tomatoes are lightly browned on top.

Added touch

Pumate, or dried Italian plum tomatoes, are used in this pasta dish – here in their oil-packed form. They are used sparingly because their concentrated tomato flavour can be overpowering. The richly flavoured oil makes a good seasoning for salad dressings or garlic bread.

Linguine with Onions

3 medium-size onions (about 350 g (12 oz) total weight)
125 ml (4 fl oz) plus 3 tablespoons olive oil
2 tablespoons fresh oregano, preferably, or other fresh herb such as marjoram or parsley
125 g (4 oz) jar sun-dried tomatoes in olive oil
125 g (4 oz) Kalamata olives
3 slices bread
Salt and freshly ground black pepper
350 g (12 oz) linguine, preferably imported

1 Peel and halve onions, then cut crosswise into thin semicircles.
2 Heat 125 ml (4 fl oz) oil in medium-size sauté pan over medium-low heat. Add onions, cover, and cook until completely softened, about 30 minutes. Do *not* allow onions to brown.
3 Meanwhile, wash fresh oregano and pat dry with paper towels. Coarsely chop enough oregano to measure 2 tablespoons. Cut sun-dried tomatoes into 5 mm (¼ inch) wide strips. Pit olives and cut lengthwise into quarters.
4 Trim off crusts from bread and discard. In food processor or with grater, grate enough bread to measure 100 g (3 oz) crumbs.
5 When olives are ready, stir in oregano, tomatoes, olives, and salt and freshly ground pepper to taste, and cook gently, uncovered, 10 minutes.
6 Meanwhile, in stockpot, bring 4 ltrs (6 pts) salted water to a boil over high heat.
7 Heat remaining 3 tablespoons olive oil in small skillet over high heat. Add bread crumbs and toss with fork until golden and toasted, about 4 minutes. Set aside.
8 Transfer onion mixture to large serving bowl.
9 Add linguine to boiling water and cook according to package directions until *al dente*.
10 Drain linguine in colander, turn into bowl with onion mixture, and toss to combine. Sprinkle with toasted bread crumbs and serve.

<table>
<tr><td>

<u>*Menu*</u>

3

</td><td>

Courgette Soup
Lamb Catanzaro-style
Broccoli Rabe

</td></tr>
</table>

The courgette soup can precede the main course of broccoli rabe and lamb chops topped with mushrooms and onions.

Whole beaten eggs thicken the courgette soup. To prevent the eggs from coagulating, first add a small portion of soup to the beaten eggs, stirring continuously. Then blend the warmed eggs into the soup. If the eggs scramble slightly despite this measure, the flavour of the soup will not be affected.

Two two-step cooking technique for the broccoli rabe is used throughout Italy. Blanching the vegetable before sautéing it eliminates any bitterness. You may substitute turnip, beet, or mustard greens, but cooking times for these greens vary, so check for doneness.

What to drink
A light red wine would best suit this menu. Choose a young Chianti, Valpolicella, or Bardolino, or a domestic Beaujolais-style Zinfandel.

Start-to-Finish Steps
1 Follow soup recipe steps 1 through 10.
2 Follow lamb recipe steps 1 through 6.
3 Follow broccoli rabe recipe steps 1 and 2.
4 Follow lamb recipe steps 7 and 8.
5 Follow broccoli rabe recipe steps 3 through 6.
6 Follow lamb recipe step 9 and broccoli rabe recipe step 7.
7 While broccoli rabe cooks, follow soup recipe steps 11 and 12, and serve.
8 Follow lamb recipe steps 10 through 12 and broccoli rabe recipe step 8, and serve.

Courgette Soup

Small bunch fresh parsley
Small bunch fresh oregano, or 2 teaspoons dried
4 medium-size courgettes (about 825 g (1¾ lb) total weight)
Medium-size onion (about 250 g (8 oz))
60 g (2 oz) pecorino Romano or Parmesan cheese
Four 2 cm (¾ inch) thick slices Italian bread
2 tablespoons lard
2 tablespoons olive oil
1 lltr (1¾ pts) beef stock
Salt
Freshly ground black pepper
2 large eggs

1 Preheat oven to 180°C (350°F or Mark 4).
2 Wash parsley and fresh oregano and dry with paper towels. Chop enough parsley to measure 15 g (½ oz). Chop enough oregano to measure 2 tablespoons. Wash courgettes, dry, and trim off ends. Cut courgettes into 1 cm (½ inch) slices. Peel and slice onion crosswise into thin rounds.
3 In food processor or with grater, grate enough cheese to measure 60 g (2 oz); set aside.
4 Arrange bread in single layer on baking sheet and toast in oven 5 minutes.
5 While bread is toasting, combine lard and olive oil in large heavy-gauge saucepan over medium heat. Add onion and sauté, stirring occasionally, 4 to 5 minutes, or until soft and translucent.
6 Turn bread and toast on other side another 5 minutes.
7 Meanwhile, bring stock to a gentle simmer in small saucepan over medium heat.
8 Add courgettes to onion and toss to combine. Add hot stock and salt and pepper to taste, and simmer gently 15 to 20 minutes, or until courgettes are tender.
9 Meanwhile, remove bread from oven and set aside. Reduce oven temperature to SLOW.
10 In medium-size bowl, combine eggs, grated cheese, and chopped herbs, and beat until blended; set aside.
11 Beating continuously with wooden spoon, slowly add 250 ml (8 fl oz) of hot soup to egg mixture; then gradually add egg mixture to soup, stirring continuously until blended. Heat soup just to a simmer; do *not* boil.
12 Place a slice of toasted bread in each of 4 soup bowls. Divide soup among bowls, and serve.

Lamb Catanzaro-style

Medium-size onion (about 250 g (8 oz))
250 g (8 oz) mushrooms
125 g (4 oz) jar capers
60 g (2 oz) anchovy fillets
125 ml (4 fl oz) plus 3 tablespoons olive oil
30 g (1 oz) plain flour, approximately
Eight 2 cm (3/4 inch) thick rib lamb chops (about
    1.25 Kg (2 1/2 lb) total weight)
Salt
Freshly ground black pepper
125 ml (4 fl oz) dry white wine

1　Peel and finely chop enough onion to
   measure 30 g (1 oz). Wipe mushrooms clean
   with damp paper towels and cut into 2 1/2 mm
   (1/8 inch) slices.
2　Rinse 2 tablespoons capers in small strainer under
   cold running water and drain. Rinse 3 anchovy
   fillets under cold running water and dry with
   paper towels. Coarsely chop capers and anchovies.
3　Heat 3 tablespoons olive oil in medium-size non-
   aluminium skillet over medium heat. Add onion
   and sauté, stirring occasionally, 5 to 8 minutes, or
   until onion is golden.
4　Meanwhile, place flour in pie pan or flat shallow
   dish. Trim off excess fat from lamb chops and dust
   chops lightly with flour.
5　Heat remaining olive oil in large heavy-gauge
   skillet over medium-high heat. Add chops and
   brown 5 to 6 minutes on one side.
6　While chops are cooking, add mushrooms, and
   salt and pepper to taste to onions, and sauté,
   stirring occasionally, 3 to 5 minutes, or until
   mushrooms release their juices.
7　Using metal tongs, turn chops and brown on other
   side another 5 to 6 minutes.
8　Cover onion-mushroom mixture, remove pan from
   heat, and set aside.
9　With slotted metal spatula, transfer chops to
   heatproof platter, sprinkle with salt and pepper,
   and place in SLOW oven.
10 Pour off all but 2 tablespoons of fat from skillet.
   Return skillet to high heat, add wine and any juices
   that have accumulated around lamb chops, and
   bring to a boil, scraping up any browned bits
   clinging to bottom of pan. Continue boiling 2 to 3
   minutes, or until liquid is reduced by half.
11 Add reduced pan juices to onion-mushroom
   mixture and stir to combine. Reheat briefly over
   medium heat.
12 Divide lamb chops among 4 dinner plates and top
   each serving with some of the onion-mushroom
   mixture.

Broccoli Rabe

Salt
750 g (1 1/2 lb) broccoli rabe or turnip, beet, or
    mustard greens
2 medium-size cloves garlic
2 lemons
4 tablespoons olive oil
Freshly ground black pepper

1　Bring 2 1/2 ltrs (4 pts) of lightly salted water to a boil
   in stockpot over high heat.
2　Meanwhile, remove tough outer leaves from
   broccoli rabe and discard. With paring knife, peel
   stems and wash broccoli rabe thoroughly under
   cold running water. Cut each stalk into thirds.

Broccoli rabe

3　Add broccoli rabe to boiling water and cook 3
   minutes.
4　While broccoli rabe is cooking, bruise garlic under
   flat blade of chef's knife and peel. Rinse 1 lemon,
   dry, and cut into 8 wedges; set aside. Halve
   remaining lemon. Squeeze juice of one half and set
   aside; reserve other half for another use.
5　Turn broccoli rabe into colander, refresh under
   cold running water, and drain. Wrap in clean
   kitchen towel or paper towels to dry.
6　Heat olive oil in large sauté pan over medium heat.
   Add garlic and sauté 2 to 3 minutes, or until lightly
   golden.
7　Add broccoli rabe, and salt and pepper to taste,
   cover pan, and cook 10 to 12 minutes, or until
   broccoli rabe is fork-tender.
8　Remove garlic and discard. Sprinkle broccoli rabe
   with lemon juice, divide among 4 dinner plates,
   and serve with lemon wedges.

Robert Pucci

Menu 1
(right)
Braised Beef Tenderloin in Wine Sauce
Potatoes Parmigiana
Sautéed Vegetables

Properly prepared Italian food is particularly wholesome and often low in fat, qualities that Robert Pucci's three menus highlight. For Menu 1, an adaptation of a restaurant meal he had in Rome, he serves an entrée of braised tenderloin steaks, mashed potatoes flavoured with grated Parmesan cheese, and a mix of fresh vegetables. Although in Italy carbohydrates are rarely eaten with the main course, mashed potatoes with braised meat are an exception.

Menu 2, an amalgam of many striking Italian flavours, begins with a Venetian-style linguine that combines freshly grated Parmesan cheese with baby clams. Flounder fillets in a zesty tomato sauce with capers and black olives (the recipe is named for Sorrento, a town near Naples) and Ligurian spinach, pine nuts, and raisins are presented after the pasta.

Well-balanced in taste, texture, and colour, Menu 3 can be planned with the angel hair pasta as the first course, followed by veal Marsala and a salad of steamed vegetables marinated in a garlic and basil vinaigrette. Or serve the salad as the appetizer and the pasta and veal together.

For an elegant dinner for company, serve individual tenderloin steaks with a creamy wine sauce, sautéed vegetables, and mashed potatoes with Parmesan and parsley.

53

Braised Beef Tenderloin in Wine Sauce
Potatoes Parmigiana
Sautéed Vegetables

Beef tenderloin steaks are served here with a cream-enriched Marsala and red wine sauce. Dry Marsalas are preferable for red meat dishes.

For the fluffiest mashed potatoes, use a high-starch potato variety such as russet. Long ovals with rough surfaces, russets – like all potatoes – should be clean, firm, and smooth without wilt, soft dark spots, a green tinge, or sprouts. Never store potatoes in the refrigerator because cold temperatures convert the starch into sugar, making the potatoes too sweet.

What to drink

The cook suggests a full-bodied Chianti Classico to complement this menu; a Spanna or Nebbiolo is also fine.

Start-to-Finish Steps

Thirty minutes ahead: Set out 125 ml (4 fl oz) heavy cream to bring to room temperature for potatoes recipe.

1 Peel and mince garlic for beef and vegetables recipes; peel garlic clove for potatoes recipe.
2 Follow potatoes recipe steps 1 through 5.
3 Follow vegetables recipe steps 1 and 2.
4 Follow potatoes recipe steps 6 through 9.
5 Follow vegetables recipe steps 3 through 7.
6 Follow beef recipe steps 1 through 9.
7 Follow vegetables recipe steps 8 through 10.
8 Follow beef recipe steps 10 through 12, potatoes recipe step 10, and serve with vegetables.

125 ml (4 fl oz) full-bodied dry red wine, such as Chianti
125 ml (4 fl oz) heavy cream, approximately

1 Preheat oven to SLOW.
2 Crush fennel seeds between 2 sheets of waxed paper with rolling pin.
3 Combine butter and oil in medium-size heavy-gauge skillet over high heat. Add steaks and cook 2 to 3 minutes per side, or until brown.
4 Using tongs, transfer steaks to platter and salt lightly. Cover loosely with foil to keep warm and set aside.
5 Reduce heat under skillet to medium-low. Stir in garlic, red pepper flakes, and crushed fennel, and cook 1 minute.
6 Add tomato paste; cook, stirring, another 2 minutes.
7 Increase heat to medium, add Marsala and red wine, and cook about 5 minutes, or until reduced by half.
8 Place 4 dinner plates in oven to warm.
9 Reduce heat under skillet to low, stir in heavy cream to taste, and cook about 5 minutes, or until sauce is thick enough to coat back of spoon.
10 Strain sauce into small bowl and return to skillet.
11 Stir in any juices that have accumulated on platter with steaks and return steaks to skillet. Over low heat, reheat steaks about 2 minutes, turning one to coat with sauce. If sauce separates, whisk in a bit more cream.
12 Place 1 steak on each dinner plate and top with sauce.

Braised Beef Tenderloin in Wine Sauce

1 tablespoon fennel seeds
2 tablespoons unsalted butter
2 tablespoons virgin olive oil
Four 2½ cm (1 inch) thick beef tenderloin steaks (about 625–750 g (1¼–1½ lb) total weight)
Salt
2 teaspoons finely minced garlic
½ teaspoon red pepper flakes
1 tablespoon tomato paste
125 ml (4 fl oz) dry Marsala, preferably Florio or Rallo

Potatoes Parmigiana

Large clove garlic, peeled
Salt
1 Kg (2 lb) boiling potatoes
Small bunch parsley
60 g (2 oz) Parmesan cheese, preferably imported
125 ml (4 fl oz) heavy cream, at room temperature
¼ teaspoon freshly grated nutmeg
Freshly ground black pepper

1 Crush garlic under flat blade of chef's knife.
2 Bring 2½ ltrs (4 pts) water, ½ teaspoon salt, and

crushed garlic to a boil in large saucepan over medium-high heat.

3 Fill large bowl half full with cold water. Peel potatoes, placing in bowl of water; cut into 2½ cm (1 inch) chunks.

4 Add potatoes to boiling water and cook 15 to 20 minutes, or until tender when pierced with a sharp knife.

5 Meanwhile, rinse parsley, dry with paper towels, and chop enough to measure 2 tablespoons. Using grater, grate cheese to measure 60 g (2 oz). Place 1 tablespoon parsley and all of the grated cheese in small bowl and toss with fork; set aside. Reserve remaining chopped parsley.

6 Drain potatoes, reserving 125 ml (4 fl oz) cooking water. Transfer potatoes to large heatproof bowl.

7 With electric mixer, beat potatoes until smooth, adding a bit reserved cooking water if they seem dry.

8 Add cream, nutmeg, and salt and pepper to taste, and beat until blended.

9 Add Parmesan and parsley and beat to combine. Adjust seasoning, cover potatoes loosely with foil, and keep warm in SLOW oven until ready to serve.

10 Divide mashed potatoes among dinner plates, sprinkle with reserved parsley, and serve.

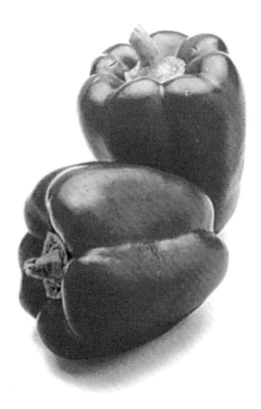

Sautéed Vegetables

250 g (8 oz) carrots
250 g (8 oz) asparagus, if available, or snow peas
125 g (4 oz) summer squash, if available
125 g (4 oz) very small courgettes, or 250 g (8 oz), if not using summer squash
1 yellow bell pepper
1 red bell pepper
Small onion
3 tablespoons unsalted butter
3 tablespoons olive oil
Large clove garlic, finely minced
1 lemon
Salt and freshly ground black pepper

1 Wash vegetables and dry with paper towels. Peel carrots and cut into 3½ cm (1½ inch) pieces. Halve pieces lengthwise and cut into 5 mm (¼ inch) thick julienne. Break off tough bottom ends of asparagus and peel, if desired. Trim off ends of summer squash and courgettes, and discard. Cut crosswise into 3½ cm (1½ inch) long pieces. Halve pieces lengthwise. Remove seeds with teaspoon and discard. Cut summer squash and courgettes into 5 mm (¼ inch) thick julienne. Halve, core, and seed bell peppers. Cut into 5 mm (¼ inch) strips. Peel and quarter onion; cut lengthwise into 2½ mm (⅛ inch) slivers.

2 In medium-size saucepan fitted with vegetable steamer, bring to a boil enough water to come just up to but not above bottom of steamer.

3 Add carrots and steam 1½ to 2 minutes, or until crisp-tender. Transfer carrots to colander, refresh under cold running water, and drain.

4 Add asparagus to pan and steam 2 to 3 minutes.

5 Transfer cooked carrots to plate and set aside.

6 Transfer asparagus to colander, refresh under cold running water, and drain.

7 Add summer squash and courgettes to pan and steam 1 minute. Transfer to colander, refresh under cold running water, and drain.

8 Combine butter and oil in large heavy-gauge skillet over medium heat. Add onion and sauté, stirring, 2 minutes. The add garlic and sauté 1 minute.

9 One at a time, add vegetables, stirring after each addition to combine, and cook 2 to 3 minutes, or just until vegetables are heated through.

10 Meanwhile, squeeze enough lemon juice to measure 1 tablespoon. Add lemon juice and salt and pepper to taste to vegetables. Turn vegetables into heatproof casserole, cover loosely with foil, and keep warm in SLOW oven until ready to serve.

<table>
<tr>
<td>

Menu

2

</td>
<td>

Linguine with Clam Sauce
Fillets of Flounder Sorrento
Sautéed Spinach with Pine Nuts and Raisins

</td>
</tr>
</table>

Baked flounder fillets in a sauce of onions, black olives, and tomatoes are accompanied by sautéed spinach with pine nuts and raisins. Mixing white and green linguine gives the pasta dish greater visual appeal.

Flounder has tender, white flesh and a delicate flavour. Select firm moist fillets with a fresh aroma, and refrigerate them well-wrapped until ready to use. To prevent sticking, coat the baking dish with sauce before adding the fish. Baking the fillets briefly keeps them from toughening. Cod, sole, or halibut are also good in this recipe.

What to drink

A crisp, dry white wine such as Verdicchio is the best choice here. Greco di Tufo and white Lacryma Christi are suitable options, as is a good French Chablis.

Start-to-Finish Steps

1 Peel and mince garlic for linguine, fish, and spinach recipes. Grate Parmesan for linguine and spinach recipes.
2 Follow fish recipe steps 1 and 2, and spinach recipe steps 1 and 2.
3 Follow fish recipe steps 3 through 5.
4 Follow spinach recipe step 3 and linguine recipe steps 1 through 5.
5 While sauce is simmering, follow fish recipe step 6.
6 Follow linguine recipe steps 6 and 7, and fish recipe step 7.
7 Follow linguine recipe step 8 and serve as first course.
8 Follow fish recipe steps 8 through 10.
9 While fish is baking, follow spinach recipe steps 4 through 6.
10 Follow fish recipe steps 11 and 12.
11 Follow spinach recipe steps 7 through 9, fish recipe step 13, and serve.

Linguine with Clam Sauce

Small bunch fresh parsley
2 tablespoons capers
Salt
2 tablespoons olive oil
4 tablespoons unsalted butter, approximately
1¹/₂ teaspoons minced garlic
300 g (10 oz) canned whole baby clams
100 ml (3 fl oz) dry white wine
350 g (12 fl oz) white and green linguine combined
60 g (2 oz) freshly grated Parmesan cheese
Freshly ground black pepper

1 Wash parsley and dry with paper towels. Chop enough to measure 4 tablespoons; reserve remainder for another use. Drain capers and chop, if large; set aside.

2 Bring 2¹/₂ ltrs (4 pts) salted water to a boil in stockpot over medium-high heat.

3 Meanwhile, combine oil and 2 tablespoons butter in large skillet over low heat. Add garlic and sauté 2 minutes.

4 Add 2 tablespoons parsley to skillet; sauté 30 seconds.

5 Strain canned clam broth into skillet; reserve clams. Stir in white wine and simmer, uncovered, 10 to 15 minutes, or until thick.

6 Add linguine to boiling water and cook 8 to 10 minutes, or according to package directions for desired doneness.

7 Add capers and clams to sauce, and simmer about 2 minutes, or just until heated through.

8 Turn pasta into colander and drain. Add pasta to sauce in skillet and toss to combine. Add Parmesan, remaining parsley, 1 or 2 tablespoons of remaining butter, and pepper to taste, and toss. Turn into large bowl and serve.

Fillets of Flounder Sorrento

Small bunch fresh oregano, or 1 teaspoon dried
Large onion
250 g (8 oz) canned Italian plum tomatoes
2 tablespoons capers
3 tablespoons olive oil
2 teaspoons minced garlic
Salt and freshly ground black pepper
30 g (1 oz) oil-cured black olives
4 fillets of flounder (625 –750 g (1–1¹/₄ lb) total weight)
125 g (4 fl oz) dry white wine

1 If using fresh oregano, wash and dry with paper towels. Chop enough to measure 1 tablespoon, reserving remainder for another use. Peel and thinly slice onion. Drain tomatoes, reserving juice for another use, and chop enough to measure 175 g (6 oz). Drain capers.

2 Heat olive oil in medium-size skillet over medium heat. Add onion and sauté, stirring occasionally, about 8 minutes, or until golden.

3 Add garlic and sauté 1 minute.

4 Add tomatoes, oregano, and salt and pepper to taste, reduce heat to medium-low, and simmer about 15 minutes, or until sauce is thickened.

5 Meanwhile, preheat oven to 230°C (450°F or Mark 8).

6 Pit olives and chop coarsely. Add olives and capers to sauce and simmer another 5 minutes.

7 Remove pan from heat, cover, and set aside.

8 Wash fillets and dry with paper towels.

9 Coat baking dish with spoonful of sauce. One at a time, arrange fillets in dish: Top each with a spoonful of sauce and then overlap with another fillet. Pour wine over fish and bake 6 to 8 minutes, or until fish flakes easily when tested with fork.

10 Place serving platter under hot water to warm.

11 When fish is done, dry platter. With wide metal spatula, gently transfer fillets with sauce to warm platter.

12 Strain pan juices into small saucepan; reduce over high heat 2 to 3 minutes, or until slightly thickened.

13 Pour reduced pan juices over fillets and serve.

Sautéed Spinach with Pine Nuts and Raisins

750 g (1¹/₂ lb) spinach
4 tablespoons unsalted butter
1 teaspoon minced garlic
2 rolled anchovies
2 tablespoons pine nuts
¹/₄ teaspoon freshly grated nutmeg
Salt and freshly ground black pepper
2 tablespoons golden raisins
2 tablespoons freshly grated Parmesan cheese

1 Remove stems from spinach and discard. Wash spinach thoroughly in several changes of cold water; do *not* dry.

2 Add spinach to stockpot and cook over medium-low heat about 5 minutes, or until wilted.

3 Turn spinach into colander, cool under cold running water, and press out excess water with back of spoon. Chop spinach coarsely; set aside.

4 Heat butter in medium-size sauté pan over low heat. Add garlic and sauté about 1 minute.

5 Add anchovies and mash into butter with back of spoon.

6 Add spinach and sauté over low heat, stirring occasionally, 5 minutes, or until moisture has evaporated. Place serving bowl under hot running water to warm.

7 Add pine nuts and nutmeg to spinach, and salt and pepper to taste; stir to combine.

8 Add raisins to mixture and continue cooking just until raisins are heated through, about 1 minute.

9 Dry serving bowl. Add Parmesan to spinach, stir to combine, and turn into warm bowl.

Angel Hair Pasta with Onions and Pepper Strips
Veal Scallopini Marsala
Warm Vegetable Salad

Veal scallops subtly flavoured with Marsala and a warm vegetable salad complement a bowl of angel hair pasta.

Veal scallopini, or scallops, are thin slices cut from the leg, which are pounded to flatten them for quick and uniform cooking. Remove any fat or filament before sprinkling the veal with flour. Scallops are best fried or sautéed briefly over medium heat so that they cook through quickly. You can also use scallops of turkey.

What to drink

Try a firm, somewhat fruity white wine, such as an Italian Chardonnay or a Tocai from Friuli.

Start-to-Finish Steps

1 Wash parsley and fresh basil, if using, and dry with paper towels. Chop enough parsley to measure 2 tablespoons for veal recipe and 2 tablespoons for pasta recipe. Chop enough basil to measure 3 tablespoons for salad recipe and refrigerate remainder for another use.
2 Follow pasta recipe steps 1 through 4.
3 Follow salad recipe steps 1 through 4.
4 Follow veal recipe steps 1 through 4.
5 Follow salad recipe step 5.
6 Follow pasta recipe steps 5 through 9, and serve as first course.
7 Follow veal recipe step 5 and salad recipe step 6.
8 Follow veal recipe step 6 and salad recipe step 7.
9 Follow veal recipe steps 7 and 8, and serve with salad.

Angel Hair Pasta with Onions and Pepper Strips

1 lemon
Small red onion
500 g (1 lb) white or yellow onions
4 tablespoons olive oil, preferably imported
3/4 teaspoon salt
1/4 teaspoon freshly ground black pepper
Pinch of sugar
1 red bell pepper
60 g (2 oz) Parmesan cheese
250 g (8 oz) angel hair pasta (capelli d'angelo) or capellini
2 to 4 tablespoons unsalted butter
2 tablespoons chopped fresh parsley

1 Wash lemon, dry, and cut in half lengthwise. With paring knife, remove peel from one half of lemon, avoiding white pith; reserve remaining half for another use.
2 Peel red onion; cut into thin slices, separate into rings, and set aside. Peel and quarter white or yellow onions; cut into thin slivers. You will have about 60 g (2 oz) red onion and about 250 g (8 oz) white or yellow onions.
3 Heat oil in heatproof casserole over low heat. Add lemon peel and sauté 2 minutes.
4 Stir in slivered onions, salt, pepper, and pinch of sugar. Raise heat to medium, cover the casserole, and simmer, stirring occasionally to prevent sticking, 20 to 30 minutes, or until onions are well browned.
5 Bring 4 ltrs (6 pts) of water to a boil over high heat.
6 Wash and dry red bell pepper. Halve, core, and seed pepper, and cut into 2 1/2 mm (1/8 inch) thick strips. Set aside. Grate Parmesan to measure 60 g (2 oz). Set aside.
7 Add pasta to boiling water and, after water returns to a boil, cook about 30 seconds for angel hair pasta or 2 to 3 minutes for capellini. Turn pasta into colander to drain.
8 Add pasta to onions in casserole and toss gently.
9 Add red onion rings, pepper strips, butter to taste, parsley, and 30 g (1 oz) grated Parmesan to pasta, and toss. Divide pasta among bowls and serve with remaining Parmesan.

Veal Scallopini Marsala

2 tablespoons vegetable oil or light olive oil
30 g (1 oz) plain flour, approximately
8 veal scallops (about 625 g (1 1/4 lb) total weight), pounded 5 mm (1/4 inch) thick
4 tablespoons unsalted butter
125 ml (4 fl oz) sweet Marsala
2 tablespoons chopped parsley

1 Preheat oven to SLOW.
2 Heat oil in large heavy-gauge skillet over medium-high heat.
3 Meanwhile, place flour in pie pan or shallow dish. One by one, dust each scallop very lightly with flour, place in skillet, and sauté about 1 minute per side. Do *not* over-crowd skillet; cook scallops in 2 batches, if necessary.
4 As they are cooked, transfer scallops to heatproof platter and keep warm in oven; wipe out skillet.
5 Place 4 dinner plates in oven to warm.
6 Add butter and Marsala to skillet and bring to a boil over high heat; continue boiling 2 to 3 minutes, or until slightly thickened.
7 Reduce heat to low. Return scallops to pan and, using tongs, turn scallops several times until well coated.
8 Divide scallops among warm plates and sprinkle each serving with parsley.

Warm Vegetable Sauce

300 g (10 oz) cherry tomatoes
250 g (8 oz) summer squash, if available
250 g (8 oz) courgettes, or 500 g (1 lb), if not using
    summer squash
250 g (8 oz) carrots
Large clove garlic
125 ml (4 fl oz) olive oil, preferably imported
2 to 3 tablespoons chopped fresh basil, or 2 to 3
    teaspoons dried
Pinch sugar
1 teaspoon salt
1/2 teaspoon freshly ground black pepper
2 tablespoons red wine vinegar, preferably imported

1 In medium-size saucepan fitted with vegetable
   steamer, bring to a boil enough water to come just
   up to but not above bottom of steamer.
2 Meanwhile, wash and dry tomatoes. Wash summer
   squash, and courgettes and discard tops and tails.
   Cut into 2 cm (3/4 inch) rounds. Peel carrots, Cut
   into 31/2 cm (11/2 inch) long pieces, and cut each
   piece lengthwise into quarters.
3 Place squash and courgettes in steamer; steam 2
   minutes.
4 Transfer squash to large heatproof bowl. Place
   carrots in steamer and steam 10 minutes.
5 Add carrots to squash, cover and keep warm in
   oven.
6 Combine oil, basil, pinch of sugar, salt, and pepper
   in small saucepan. Put garlic through press, add to
   mixture in pan, and cook over low heat for 4
   minutes.
7 Stir in vinegar and pour warm dressing over
   vegetables. Add whole cherry tomatoes and toss to
   combine.

Added touch
For this creamy ricotta pudding, use imported Italian
candied citrus peel if possible. If peel is unavailable,
increase the mixture of dark and golden raisins and
currants proportionately.

Ricotta Pudding

2 tablespoons candied citrus peel
1 tablespoon dark raisins
1 tablespoon golden raisins
1 tablespoon currants
60 ml (2 fl oz) brandy or fruit-flavored liqueur
4 large eggs, at room temperature, separated
100 g (3 oz) granulated sugar
750 g (11/2 lb) ricotta or cottage cheese
Grated peel of 1 lemon
1/2 teaspoon vanilla extract
2 tablespoons all-purpose flour
Salt
1 tablespoon unsalted butter, approximately
30 g (1 oz) dried bread crumbs, approximately
Confectioners' sugar

1 Preheat oven to 180°C (350°F or Mark 4).
2 Chop candied citrus peel and combine with raisins,
   and currants, and brandy in a small bowl. Set aside
   to soak at least 15 minutes.
3 If using food processor, combine egg yolks, sugar,
   cheese, lemon peel, and vanilla, and process until
   combined. Add flour and process until blended. If
   using electric mixer, first combine yolks and sugar,
   and beat until thoroughly blended before adding
   cheese, flavourings, and flour.
4 Add brandy but not fruit to the mixture and blend;
   then add the fruit and blend briefly to combine.
5 Beat egg whites with a pinch of salt until stiff. Pour
   one third of cheese mixture over egg whites and
   gently fold in until totally incorporated.
6 Generously butter 11/2 ltr (3 pt) soufflé dish. Add
   bread crumbs and evenly coat dish.
7 Turn pudding into prepared dish and place in
   baking pan. Fill pan with enough hot water to
   come halfway up sides of soufflé dish and bake 60
   to 70 minutes, or until pudding is nicely browned.
8 Remove pudding from oven and let stand in water
   bath 30 minutes before unmoulding.
9 To unmould, run thin-bladed knife around edge of
   soufflé dish. Place large flat plate upside down
   over dish and, holding plate and dish firmly
   together, turn upside down. If pudding does not
   unmould, rap plate and dish once against hard
   surface. Remove soufflé dish.
10 Sprinkle pudding with confectioners' sugar and
   serve.

Meet the Cooks

Silvana La Rocca

The daughter of an Italian diplomat, Silvana La Rocca was born and raised in the Abruzzo region of central Italy. Although she holds a Master's Degree in international law, Silvana La Rocca cooks for a living. She resides in California, where she operates a delicatessen, take-out and catering business.

Felice and Lidia Bastianich

Felice Bastianich and his wife, Lidia, were born in Istria, but met and married in New York. They opened their first restaurant in Queens in 1970 and now own and operate Felidia in Manhattan, which features authentic Italian regional food with a focus on Istrian dishes.

Lynne Kasper

Cooking teacher and food writer Lynne Kasper has studied with many leading cooks and at L'Ecole de Cuisine La Varenne in Paris. She is a founding member of the International Association of Cooking Schools and a regular contributor to magazines. She now lives in Brussels where she teaches cookery.

Susan DeRege

Born in Ontario, Canada, Susan DeRege is married to a native of Piedmont, Italy. She has travelled throughout northern Italy gathering unusual and authentic recipes and has worked as a test-kitchen home economist.

Nancy Verde Barr

A specialist in southern Italian cookery, Nancy Barr studied at Modern Gourmet in Massachusetts. She has taught cooking in France and at the Chefs Company Cooking School in Rhode Island.

Robert Pucci

Robert Pucci lives in Austin, Texas, and runs Pasta by Pucci, a catering business that specializes in Italian cooking. Besides catering, he works as a cook for several families. Interested in food since childhood, he lived in Italy for a year, studying and sampling the country's regional dishes.

A Wealth of Herbs

Increasingly, herbs are arriving in the markets fresh; the proliferation of health stores and other specialist shops has widened choice, and many cooks with gardens have taken to raising their own. Recent ethnic influences have called attention to once seemingly esoteric herbs. Coriander, for one, is at last gaining deserved popularity in Europe, although cooks in Asia and the Middle East have been using it for centuries.

Anyone wishing to dry fresh herbs can tie them loosely in a bundle and hang them upside down in a cool, dark, well-ventilated place for several weeks. When the leaves are completely dried, strip them from the stems and store them in an airtight container.

Two swifter methods of preserving herbs make use of the microwave oven and the freezer. To microwave herbs, place five or six sprigs at a time between paper towels and microwave them on high for 1 to 3 minutes until the leaves are brittle. Store the leaves loosely in airtight jars.

To freeze herbs, rinse the sprigs and pat them dry. Strip the leaves off the stems and put them into a heavy-duty plastic bag. Gently flatten the bag to force out the air, seal the bag tightly, and place it in your freezer. Use the leaves as the need arises.

Basil (also called sweet basil): This fragrant herb, its underlying flavour of anise and hint of clove, particularly well with tomato.

Chervil: The small, lacy leaves of this herb have a akin to parsley with a touch of anise. It is good i ads and salad dressings. Chervil is popular in Fr where it is often an ingredient in herb mixtures, in ing *fines herbes*. When used in cooking, chervil sh be added at the end, lest its subtle flavour be lost

Chives: The smallest of the onions, chives grow in g clumps. When finely cut, the hollow leaves contri their delicate, oniony flavour to fresh salads and vegetables. Chives should always be used fresh, as ones are virtually tasteless.

Coriander (also called cilantro): The serrated leav the coriander plant impart a distinctive fragrance a flavour that is both mildly sweet and bitter. Coria leaves should be used fresh or added at the en cooking if their flavour is to be appreciated fully.

Dill: A sprightly herb with feathery leaves, dill enha cucumber and many other fresh vegetables, as we fish and shellfish. When used in cooking, dill shoul added towards the end of the process to preserv delicate flavour. Both dill seeds and dill leaves ca